D1572292

THE
DIVERSITY
ADVANTAGE

A Guide to Making
Diversity Work

THIRD EDITION

THE
DIVERSITY
ADVANTAGE

A Guide to Making Diversity Work

Lenora Billings-Harris

The Diversity Advantage *Third Edition* by Lenora Billings-Harris

Copyright © 2013 by Lenora Billings-Harris All Rights Reserved.

ISBN: 978-0-9710948-6-4

Published by: Somerville Press, Greensboro NC

Library of Congress Control Number: 2012940072

Copy-Editor: Tiffany Taylor

Interior Design: Christopher Derrick

Cover design by Pat Theriault

First Printing: August 2013

12 13 14 15 16 17 18 10 9 8 7 6 5 4 3 2 1

Printed in the United States of America

To: All of my ancestors whose shoulders I stand upon, who through their struggles and victories made my life possible.

*To: Those to come,
who will follow the path of creating a world that honors, values and celebrates difference, and who will continue the journey to find ways for people to accept difference without resorting to violence.*

TABLE OF CONTENTS

PREFACE

ACKNOWLEDGMENTS

PREFACE

As I PEN THIS PREFACE, I am thinking about September 11, and the attack on United States. Across the world last year, there were observances of the 10th anniversary of the attack. As we all reflect on that shocking day, I think about how much has changed in what is now eleven years later and how much has not yet changed as it relates to understanding and respecting differences. 9/11 made us think about our freedoms, and it also ignited new stereotypes and biases based on fear. Islamophobia has entered our lexicon of diversity-related words. As a nation we knew we could not take the feeling of being safe for granted ever again, thus many people still blame all Muslims for the attack. Doing so, even though misguided, is a way for some to manage their pain.

The first edition of this book was published in 1998. Much has changed since then within the diversity and inclusion space both in the USA as well as around the globe. Just as most people never imagined an attack on the homeland of the USA, most also never imagined an African American president with a last name of Obama, or that Facebook and Twitter could fuel the power of ordinary people to make extraordinary demands for liberty around the world. We never imagined a world-wide financial crisis, or constant floods, tornados, tsunamis, and hurricanes at devastating proportions, or women, Asian, Latin, and African American CEO's of Fortune 500 corporations such as American Express, PepsiCo, Sunoco, Aetna, DuPont, and others. We never imagined a Latina Supreme Court Justice named Sonia Sotomajor.

Change has been frightening, frustrating and fabulous at the same time.

I am often asked why I do this work (diversity and inclusion). My brief answer is that I am constantly overcome by humankind's ability to hate. I am overwhelmed by the rationale people use as permission to hate and hurt others for no reason other than that those "others" are different; different races and ethnicities, different faiths and beliefs, different sexual orientations and identities, different ages, different attitudes and politics, different personalities, different abilities, and so on.

I am driven to do something in whatever way that I can, to help us all learn and understand at a deep level that hate comes from fear and fear often is fueled by the belief that we will lose something. We fear that which we do not understand. So, the more we can understand different points of view and recognize that they are just different not wrong, perhaps the sooner we can all channel our energies toward building on those differences to find better solutions to the problems of the world. This enables us to gain much and lose little.

When we hate just because of a difference, we steal away our ability to discover new solutions. On the other hand, when we challenge ourselves to look for the facts and commonalities, we can then place blame for crimes and other deplorable behavior where it is due, instead of spreading the blame to all people of any one group.

Understanding does not come to us without commitment to lean into our fears with the belief that on the other side of that fear are answers to help us make better decisions about ourselves and others. I am inspired by the many people, though not enough people, who are willing to speak up to stop bullying, racism, homophobia, sexism and socio-economic disenfranchisement.

My hope is that the following pages will inspire you to become part of the solution by determining ways to contribute to a heightened understanding of people different from you. The world needs people who respect difference, and who seek understanding instead of blame. This book is filled with tips, techniques, and ideas that any individual can apply to this end.

Join with me to take personal responsibility for making a difference within each of our spheres of influence at work, at home, within our communities large and small by speaking up, by asking questions and really listening instead of remaining silent and expecting others to step up. It does take a village, and each village is filled with individuals like you. Each of us can make a difference. Join this Solution Revolution to make Diversity an Advantage.

ACKNOWLEDGMENTS

THANK YOU TO ALL WHO read, purchased, shared, and used this book in earlier versions as teaching tools, and organizational guides. Because of you this book continues to be relevant, and I continue to be motivated to update it. Because of the sensitive topic, many who contributed their experiences remain nameless on the following pages. I thank the hundreds of participants who were willing to share their stories and their pain so others could understand the importance of the subject of valuing diversity and engaging all people, instead of a select few.

Thank you to my editors, Gerald Hedlund, Jen Marshall, and the staff of Advantage Books for their undying patience, and for providing such professional assistance at every step of the process.

I thank Natasha Toussaint for her research, and Damaris Paterson for her generational diversity insights and contributions.

Without the constant support and unselfish guidance from experienced authors, most of whom are members of the National Speakers Association, I never would have believed in myself as an author. Special thanks to Chris Clarke-Epstein, Tracy Brown, Ed Scannell, Dr. Julianne Malveaux, and Glenna Salsbury.

And lastly, yet most importantly, I thank Charles, my husband of over thirty-seven years. Your love, support, patience, vision, critiques and most of all encouragement make this incredible career of writing, speaking, and consulting possible. You are the wind beneath my wings.

.

UBUNTU
Translation: *I am because we are.*
We are because I am.

— **South African Proverb**

CHAPTER 1

WHAT *is* DIVERSITY *in the* WORKPLACE?

A Historical Perspective

Remember always that you have not only the right to be an individual, you have an obligation to be one. You cannot make any useful contribution in life unless you do this.

— Eleanor Roosevelt

ROBERT, FAHEEM, TRACEE, Kewal, Lois, Hernando, and Dorothy are account executives for a small but rapidly growing company.

Their ages range from 23 to 59 years old; two are single, two are married; three have life partners; three are child-free, three are parents; one is gay and one is blind; one is caring for a parent and two children; two are single parents. There are four languages and six religions represented by this group. This is diversity in the workplace.

The word *diversity* simply means differences or variety. As used when referring to the American workplace, diversity refers to the many differences present among workers today. Diversity in the workplace includes all of the ways people are different, not only differences in ethnicity, age, gender, and ability so often thought of as part of EEOC (Equal Employment Opportunity Commission) regulations.

Workforce 2000, in a report published by the Hudson Institute in 1987, predicted that 83% of new entrants to the labor market would be individuals other than able-bodied white males by the year 2000. This report also predicted that 50% of the labor market would be older than 50 by that time. The study went on to predict that by the year 2050, 47% of all Americans will be other than European American (White).

A study conducted by the *Population Reference Bureau* in 2005 found that 69.6% of the workforce population was white, non- Hispanic, 13.3% were Hispanic, and 17.1% were other non- Hispanic. This study also predicted that by 2050, 51.4% of workers will be white, non-Hispanic, 24.3% will be Hispanic, and 24.3% will be other, non-Hispanic.

The changes that are predicted will be dramatic in the next forty years. The predictions made in 1987 are on track. Diversity has certainly become an important focus in the workplace. Among individual populations, however, the participation of each cultural background is relatively the same, averaging between 76% and 87% of their populations involved in the workforce.

The diversity movement as we know it today began in earnest due to the above projections as well as several others included in the Hudson Institute's *Workforce 2000* report. Progressive organizations recognized that their employees of the future would have different needs, expectations, and values than those possessed by the leaders of the company. While the projections may not have come true, the trend remains and that makes it more important than ever for companies to be culturally diverse.

In order to attract the best talent, companies began to evaluate their culture, their norms, and their expectations with regard to acculturating people who are different. In addition to the workplace looking different, another startling statistic was revealed originally in the *Workforce 2000* report. The labor market would be considerably smaller than it had been in the past (labor market = new entrants into the workforce). Because baby boomers had fewer children than previous generations, there simply are fewer people available to work today. Companies are already experiencing huge competition for attracting the best talent.

These demographics present opportunities and challenges.

Since 1987, many organizations have gone through downsizing, right- sizing, re-engineering, and other euphemistic terms for terminating employees. Thus, those who remain often feel there is not enough time, not enough resources, and too much work to do per employee. This added level of stress, compounded by getting things done through working in teams, has created more opportunity for diversity collisions. Too often, organizations have grouped people to- gether and called them a team, when in fact they are still simply a group of individuals, not a team working together.

Once individuals learn to respect differences of others, the work teams become more highly productive and innovative, and they often make fewer costly mistakes. A diverse workforce can assist organizations in their efforts to penetrate emerging markets, attract and retain the best talent, improve customer relations, and reduce employee complaints and grievances. All of these challenges and opportunities have strong bottom-line implications.

Organizations that have taken the initiative to include diversity and inclusion as one of their business focuses have developed many diversity definitions and mission statements. As a basis for discussion throughout this book, I will use the following definitions:

Valuing Workforce Diversity: Having the willingness and the ability to recognize, understand, respect, and utilize the contributions of all individuals, regardless of their packaging.

Leveraging Diversity: Having the ability and willingness to create and sustain an environment of respect, where all
employees can reach their highest level of productivity, thus contributing to the success of the organization.

More recently progressive organizations are also focusing on employee engagement. I believe diversity, inclusion, and engagement are intertwined, thus engagement will often be mentioned in this book.

Gallup conducted extensive research connecting engagement to organizational financial outcomes. The following is a combination of their definition along with others:

Employee Engagement: A Leading Indicator of Financial Performance
It is a strategic foundation for the way progressive organizations do business. They are more productive, profitable, more customer-focused, safer, and more likely to withstand temptations to leave. The best- performing companies know that an employee engagement improvement strategy linked to the achievement of corporate goals will help them win in the marketplace.

Employee engagement goes beyond satisfaction and ensures the long- term and productive tenure of the faithful employee with the employer. It is satisfaction, commitment, pride, loyalty, sense of personal responsibility, and willingness to be an advocate for the organization that have an impact on behavior.

As you read this book, continue to ask yourself, "How does the diverse environment affect me?" Allow yourself to explore its advantages and tackle personal challenges.

Making a Difference

1. What have you noticed in your community and your workplace that reflects a growing change in demographics?

> Multilingual voting ballots.
> Discounts for seniors.
> Two-income families.
> Single parents.
> Home-based businesses.
> Assigned parking slots for the physically challenged.
> TV programming varied rather than having stereotypical roles for certain actors.
> Women present in all types of positions. (There is really no such thing as a non-traditional job anymore for women or men.)
> People with disabilities more visible in all walks of life.
> Concern for political correctness.
> A variety of ethnic restaurants available.
> Telecommuting.
> More variety in the types of places of worship available.
> List others:

2. What challenges have these changes caused for you?
3. What benefits have you observed or experienced as a result of diversity in your community and workplace?

Articles and Webinars
http://goo.gl/U3fTPO
http://goo.gl/7ZwdeL

CHAPTER 2

WHY SHOULD I CARE ABOUT DIVERSITY?

How Does It Affect My Job Day-to-Day?

*If a man is offered a fact which goes against
his instincts, he will scrutinize it closely, and
unless the evidence is overwhelming, he will
refuse to believe it.
If, on the other hand, he is offered something
which affords a reason for acting in accordance
to his instincts, he will accept it.*

— Bertrand Russell

HAVE YOU EVER HAD A clash with one of your staff members? Have any of your staff avoided or complained about working with another team member?

Most of the clashes or *diversity collisions* that occur at work happen because the individuals involved are unable or unwilling to recognize and value differences. The natural inclination is to judge differences. When a reason for the conflict cannot be readily identified, stereotypical beliefs or biases are often used to rationalize the cause.

Imagine that you supervise Wendell, who is a European American man, and Fatima, who is an African American woman. Both Fatima and Wendell have great ideas regarding ways to improve customer relations. They each, separately, have shared some of their ideas with you. Given that you want your employees to work well together in teams, you decide to assign the two of them to work together on a special project. Their assignment is to identify ways to improve customer service and develop an implementation plan. What you don't know is that Wendell and Fatima don't get along very well. Here's what could happen:

The report is due next Monday. It is now Wednesday. Because neither employee really wants to be around the other, they procrastinate until

Friday. Finally, Fatima goes to Wendell's workstation to begin brainstorming this project. Every idea that Wendell shares, Fatima criticizes. Each time Fatima begins to share an idea, Wendell interrupts her. This behavior continues for 15 or 20 minutes. If these two adults were thinking logically and were really interested in solving this conflict, one or the other would eventually stop this interaction and analyze the process to determine how to improve it. Wendell might say, "Fatima, I appreciate that you so easily see the negatives in ideas. This can, sometimes, be beneficial because it helps people avoid errors. I would appreciate it, however, if you would look for the positives in my ideas as well."

Fatima, if she were thinking logically, might say to Wendell, "Please, let me complete my statements before you respond. When you interrupt, I find it difficult to continue my train of thought in a non-defensive manner."

In other words, each individual would develop a contract with the other and come to an agreement on how best to work with each other in order to complete the project. This type of positive conflict resolution rarely ever happens in the workplace.

Everyone is already under stress due to a lack of resources, lack of time, and sometimes lack of skill in dealing with these types of issues.

The two of them decide to meet on Monday morning. As they each get in their car to drive home, they could have the following thoughts:

Wendell is talking to himself in anger. "Why do I have to work with Fatima? She's a pushy, Black broad who thinks she knows everything. She's always on the defensive and she's probably suffering from PMS." Now, of course, all of Wendell's thoughts are stereotypical. It is possible that they could be true when applied to Fatima, but more likely he isn't talking about Fatima as an individual at all. The stereotypes are simply an easy excuse for the reasons they are ineffective when working together.

Fatima is driving home as well and her thoughts are no better. She says to herself, "This will never work. I'll never be able to complete this project successfully with Wendell. After all, he's a middle-aged, White guy. Certainly he cannot deal with an assertive, professional Black woman such as myself. Plus, men never listen to women anyway. They're always interrupting. If it's not their idea, it's not a good idea." Fatima relies on stereotypes to generalize and rationalize why she is having a conflict with Wendell.

Monday morning they must meet again because they have not completed the project. They suffer through this process and eventually create a two or three-page report for you. Is it their best work? That's doubtful. Has their productivity been affected? Of course. Have they resolved the conflict? No. Their stereotypes are based on past messages received over their lifetime, and perhaps a few direct experiences.

The stereotypes were just waiting in the background to be snatched up and applied to the first conflict situation. As you read this tale, you might say to yourself, "I just don't think that way." However, remember that you are probably in your logical state of mind at this moment, as you are reading this book.

Stereotypes tend to surface when you are stressed, afraid, or otherwise emotionally distressed. Most people rely on stereotypes, although it is often unconscious, because it is easier than resolving the conflict, and those chosen seem to fit.

Diversity affects you with each encounter with another person. You are a culture of one; there is no one else just like you. Your differences or uniqueness can add to the strength of the organization if the environment is one that encourages recognition of differences and supports strategies and techniques to build on those differences in a harmonious way.

Making a Difference

Think of someone with whom you have a conflict. What specific behaviors does this person act out that affect you negatively?

List everything the two of you have in common.

In what ways are the two of you very different? Include such things as age, ethnicity, gender, title, work location or department, education, and so on.

Is it possible that stereotypical beliefs or biases are creating barriers to your effectiveness? (Be brutally honest. No one will see this except you.)

Identify the positive attributes of this individual. How can these attributes make your team stronger?

Take the first step. Have a conversation with this individual to resolve the conflict. (See chapter 16 to learn how to give feedback in a negative situation.)

Articles and Webinars
http://goo.gl/U3fTPO
http://goo.gl/7ZwdeL

CHAPTER 3

WHAT *is the* DIFFERENCE BETWEEN DIVERSITY *and* EEO/AFFIRMATIVE ACTION?

You can't hold a man down without staying down with him.
— Booker T. Washington

OVER THE PAST TWENTY years, many organizations have renamed their Equal Employment Opportunity (EEO)/Affirmative Action efforts "diversity initiatives." This has often been a mistake. Although EEO, Affirmative Action, and diversity are connected in their focus on inclusion, they are very different in their reason for existence. Because people have developed strong opinions about EEO/Affirmative Action and its usefulness, renaming these efforts as diversity has made many people immediately oppose any initiatives. Renaming did not defuse the red flag response to these regulations.

Affirmative Action regulations require that an organization develop goals for hiring and promoting people who are within "protected classes." However, many people within the organization see these goals as quotas. Quotas are perceived as "ceilings"; when we achieve the quota, we can stop. Goals are perceived as "floors"; when we achieve a goal, we set a higher one.

Let's take a look at each of the three elements: Equal Employment Opportunity, Affirmative Action, and diversity.

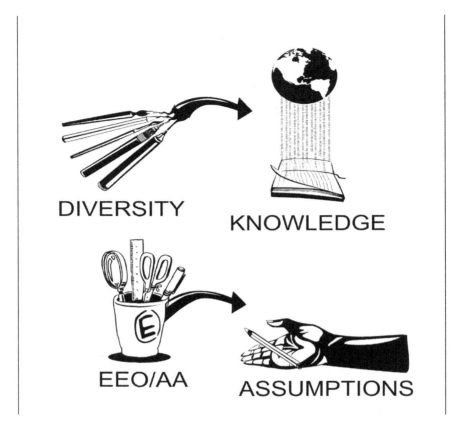

Equal Employment Opportunity

Equal Employment Opportunity (EEO) refers to government-mandated regulations targeted toward organizations with 100 or more employees. (Go to www.eeoc.gov for the full statement regarding compliance.) These regulations were introduced as part of Title VII of the Civil Rights Act of 1964, which originally focused its efforts on creating opportunities in the workplace primarily for African Americans and women. "Protected classes" include people of color; women; people with disabilities (Americans with Disabilities Act of 1990); Vietnam War veterans; individuals of a religion; age; national origin; and others. In reality, everyone is protected under this act. The primary focus of EEO has been to create equal hiring, development, and promotion opportunities for those who, in the past, were discriminated against because of the cultural group to which they were a member.

These regulations require that employers provide an equal opportunity for "protected class" individuals to apply for positions and an equal chance to be considered for promotion. For example, soon after the regulations were introduced, employers discontinued the practice of identifying jobs as "for women" or "for men" in the classified section of the newspaper. Theoretically, job applications from people in the protected classes would be accepted by employers and considered equally along with those of White male classification. Unfortunately, change was slow. Thus, Affirmative Action was introduced as a result of Presidential Executive Order 11246, signed by Lyndon B. Johnson in 1965.

Affirmative Action

Affirmative Action (AA) requires some businesses to create and maintain a workforce whose demographics match the community within which the business is located. If this is not the case, organizations are required to develop Affirmative Action plans that specifically identify what steps will be taken yearly to attract underrepresented people to the organization. Many companies became more visible as recruiters on campuses of HBCU's (Historically Black Colleges and Universities), placed ads in ethnic newspapers and magazines and became supporters of nonprofit organizations such as the Urban League in order to meet the requirements of Affirmative Action regulations.

The general assumption was that if enough "different" people worked together on a daily basis, racism, sexism, ageism, and the like, would eventually disappear from American society. It has not worked, even though many people were, and are, allowed to work within organizations that would not have opened their doors otherwise without this government intervention.

Affirmative Action admission practices of institutions of higher education have been challenged in the courts. One of the most recognized cases was the Supreme Court ruling in 2003 that upheld the admissions policies of The University of Michigan Law School.

However, courts have ruled on both sides of this issue, and the debate continues.

Some organizations felt their work was done once a "person of difference" was hired. Little or no attention had been given to how people were treated once they were hired. It was expected that once given the opportunity to join the organization, people were to assimilate themselves into the organization's norms, values, and behaviors, even if that meant they must deny their own cultural strengths. They were expected to sacrifice their individuality as it related to differences from the majority (i.e., ethnicity, gender, religion, etc.) and act as much like those in power as possible, if they expected to get ahead.

From the mid-70's through the mid-80's, in order to succeed in the corporate world, for example, women knew they should dress as much like men as possible. Many wore silk bow ties, dark suits, white blouses, and conservative jewelry, and cut their hair or pulled it back so it did not touch their shoulders. Corporate rationale was such that if women dressed in a feminine way, they would be too distracting on the job. It did not work. Men still noticed that women were women. More important, women should not have been held accountable for men's behavior. Although many women choose to dress very conservatively today, most progressive organizations recognize that attire does not, by itself, predict talent or potential. Additionally, the male uniform of dark suit, white shirt, and clean-shaven face has begun to fade as required attire for many jobs. Casual days and business casual dress has become the norm in many organizations.

The United States has been referred to as a melting pot, which implied that individuals must give up their uniqueness and wear a facade in order to get ahead. The rule was that you should not flaunt your differences. A melting pot is like a stew that cooks a long time. In the end, the flavor might be good but you cannot identify the individual ingredients. Everything loses its original identity and its unique strength.

In May, 2009, the first Hispanic Supreme Court justice was appointed. Judge Sonya Sotomayor has been an advocate for considering race and ethnicity in university admissions, hiring, and judicial selection and her appointment means that there will be more serious debate regarding affirmative action in the future.

Diversity

At about the same time businesses were realizing that they were spending a great deal of time and money recruiting women and other under-represented groups but doing a poor job of retaining them, the Hudson Institute published its study of the labor trends in the United States. The U.S. Department of Labor needed to determine what the demographics of the labor market would be by the year 2000 and commissioned this study, which was later supplemented and updated with a U.S. Labor Force Study in 2005. It was the findings of these reports, Workforce 2000 and U.S. Labor Force Trends, coupled with the realization that putting people together who are different does not mean they will automatically work well together, that began the diversity movement. (Note: In 2011, Hudson Institute published Workforce 2020.)

As organizations began to implement diversity initiatives, their motivations for actions were, and are, different than actions caused by EEO and Affirmative Action. Diversity initiatives are incorporated into the organization for one of three motivations:

   a. Senior management believes it is the right thing to do.
   b. The organization is losing money due to discrimination and sexual harassment lawsuits and/or high turnover.
   c. Recognizing and respecting differences enables teams to be more highly productive, and employees more engaged.

Progressive organizations recognize that their worker demographics will be, and in many cases already are, very different than they were 20 or even 10 years ago. If businesses plan to be successful, they must start now by reexamining how they treat people, all people, employed within their company.

Because diversity initiatives are not a government mandate or regulation, there are no "protected classes." Businesses are motivated to initiate inclusive policies and practices because they foresee a bottom-line payoff. They are recognizing that the diversity of their employees adds to their strength in the marketplace, when diverse people are included at all levels. The more an organization "looks like" the market it serves, the more likely people will want to do business with them and work for them.

The values and expectations of organizational leadership are often very different than the values and expectations of the new worker. For example, many Generation X'ers and Millenials (Gen Y) generally value quality of life issues more strongly than Baby Boomers and Mature workers did when they were young. Many choose where they plan to live first, then search for a job in that location, rather than moving to wherever the job is, as Baby Boomers and Matures did. It is no longer expected practice that within many organizations you must be ready to move your family every two years in order to succeed. Companies are finding innovative ways to retain talented, skilled workers because they run the risk of losing them to competitors if they ignore these important values. Workers today are proud of their ethnic heritage and do not choose to hide or diminish it, as was expected in the past. Employees expect to be allowed to celebrate their religious holidays and wear religious attire to work.

Leaders today are confronted with these and other difficult challenges unlike they ever had to consider before. Just as predicted in Workforce 2000 and reconfirmed in Workforce 2020, the labor pool is shrinking.

They wrestle with issues such as business casual attire, visible tattoos, and facial piercing as it relates to job performance because talent is scarce and it comes in all types of "packaging."

Thus, diversity celebrates differences instead of hiding or trying to change them. The more diverse a work team is, the more effective it can be if the team members respect each other's differences and value the contributions of those who are different. The challenge of leading a diverse organization is how to help workers feel valued and respected as individuals while helping everyone focus on the mission and goals of the organization.

When valuing diversity, the United States has been referred to as a "tossed salad" or "stir-fry." It has fruits and nuts along with vegetables, and each ingredient maintains its uniqueness while contributing to the overall flavor and value of the salad or stir-fry. The ingredients do not lose their identity in order to contribute, and the first bite of the salad does not taste like the last bite. All are unique.

Making a Difference

1. To develop a deeper understanding of Equal Employment Opportunity and Affirmative Action, contact your local EEO office. Every city and state has such an office. It is this office that enforces the EEO and Affirmative Action regulations.

2. To identify what diversity initiatives your company may have undertaken, contact your company's Human Resources Department, or your chief diversity officer. Dis-

cuss this with your manager and ask what initiatives are in place and how you can help support them.

3. Actions you can take to demonstrate your support of the diversity advantage within your work group:

4. Mentor a new employee.

5. Show intolerance of stereotypical comments, jokes, gestures, and the like.

6. Evaluate others based on facts rather than judging based on bias or stereotypical beliefs.

Articles and Webinars
http://goo.gl/U3fTPO
http://goo.gl/7ZwdeL

CHAPTER 4

WHAT *are the* CORRECT TERMS *and* WHY MUST I CHANGE MY WORDS?

Please don't say I'm 'wheelchair-bound' or even worse, 'confined to a wheelchair.

— Rolf Hotchkiss

ARE YOU TIRED OF POLITICAL correctness and wonder why it is suggested that language should become more sensitive? As our society and workplaces continue to expand their diversity, more and more people want to be referred to by terms they have chosen rather than the labels selected by others. Sometimes the power of words is underestimated.

Thus, one ill-chosen word can create friction between people.

Many people with Latino heritage, for example, do not like the term *Hispanic* because it was a term formulated by the United States Census Bureau in 1970. When it was realized that many U.S. households consisted of families who spoke Spanish, there had not previously been a way to record this. Rather than attempt to identify every country from which these residents' ancestors might have come, the Census Bureau created the word *Hispanic*. Hispanic is not really an ethnic group. It is a generalized term used to describe a diverse group of people whose primary language is often Spanish.

On the other hand, some people of Latino heritage prefer the term *Hispanic* because they believe it carries less bias than the words *Mexican* or *Puerto Rican,* for example.

Many Blacks prefer *African American* because the word *black* is rarely capitalized, even when it is specifically referring to that ethnic group (except within books written by African Americans and magazines targeting the African American culture), whereas *African American* does have the honor of capital letters. Some people believe the small case "b" is another example of subtle, institutionalized racism. African American is a term of pride. Unlike European Americans who can choose to recognize their Irish, German, or Italian heritage, African Americans do not have that option for recognizing their specific heritage. For many African Americans it is impossible to identify their ancestors' country of origin. On the other hand, some Blacks do not like *African American* because they see themselves as American and not African since Africa is not a country; it is a continent. Each time I visit South Africa to work with organizations there, I am acutely aware that I am American, even though I am proud of my African heritage.

One person can never know all of the right words to use. However, when a reference must be made, ask people who are members of that group which term they prefer. The answers will vary. People have individual preferences, but your interest in asking questions will demonstrate your effort to show respect. Too often we assume, instead of asking, thus causing misunderstandings and conflicts. Perhaps a more effective way of referring to different ethnic groups is to place the word *American* in front of the ethnicity; for example, Americans of European heritage, Americans with Asian heritage, Americans with Latino heritage, and so on.

Although using words and phrases that show respect and sensitivity requires effort, it really is not very difficult or time-consuming. The following list highlights words and terms that can be substituted for less respectful terms. Note that some phrases do not have a more acceptable alternative and should be eliminated from use altogether.

The list on the next page is extreme in order to provide the most useful alternatives. Recognize that you will never make 100% of your colleagues happy. Pick a few words/phrases that you are able to change, thus showing your desire to connect with and respect others who differ from you.

Words You Can Lose	Words You Can Use
Black sheep	Outcast
Guys (when referring to a mixed group)	Friends; folks
You people	You
Oriental (when referring to people)	Asian (using specific nationality, e.g. Korean is even better when possible)
Acting like wild Indians	Unruly
Girls (when referring to female adults)	Women
Policeman/Postman	Police officer/mail carrier
"Calling a spade a spade"	Telling it like it is...

Your husband/wife (in a general context)	Spouse/partner
Handicapped	People with special needs physically/mentally challenged; people with disabilities; people with limitations
Retarded	People/Person with special needs
Gifted children	Advanced learners
Race	Ethnicity or nationalit
Uneducated(when referring to adults)	Lacking formal education
The little woman; the wife	Your wife; his wife; my wife
"Don't go postal on me!"	Don't lose your temper
Acting blonde	Unintelligent
Old people	Seniors; mature
Bitchy	Aggressive/assertive
"White" lie	Lie
Homosexual	LGBT
Church (when speaking in general terms)	Place of worship
Jew down	Negotiate
Blacklisted	Banned
"Manning" the project	Staffing the project
Chop Chop	Move quickly
Is or is not "black and white"	Is or is not clear or abosolue

Making a Difference

It is impossible to constantly know what words show the most sensitivity, and when and how to use the most sensitive words all the time. Since "appropriate" words change all the time, try using the following suggestions:

1. Ask several people within the same cultural group which terms they prefer.
2. Omit slang terms when referring to others.
3. Do not use derogatory terms to describe others even if people within the cultural group do. For example, if a Jewish person tells a joke about Jews that is not per- mission for others not in the group to do the same. The use of specific derogatory terms by a group that aren't acceptable coming from another group has become a big issue during these past ten years. For example, the "N" word, as used by rap and hip hop artists and now youths in general across the country is another example. When Black kids call each other this, it's fine (to some), but when a White person says it, they are called racist. Doing this is confusing to those not in the group, and it perpetuates the inappropriate behavior.
4. Refrain from joking about a person's bald head, size, or lack of height. Even if they politely laugh, it does not mean they think it is funny.
5. Lighten up, and show respect at the same time. Be will- ing to say, "I'm sorry," or "I didn't mean to offend." Most people will recognize your sincerity, if it is truly present.

Article
How To Refer To Ethnicity In A Sensitive Way
http://goo.gl/YrQCyF

CHAPTER 5

HOW CAN I INCREASE MY KNOWLEDGE *about* VARIOUS CULTURAL GROUPS *so that* I DO NOT RELY *on* BIASED *and* STEREOTYPED INFORMATION?

Knowledge of [another] culture should sharpen our ability to scrutinize more steadily, to appreciate more lovingly, our own.

— Margaret Mead

THERE ARE FOUR CORNERstones of Diversity that, if developed, can help to create an inclusive, respectful, and productive working environment.

Knowledge

Acceptance

Understanding

Behavior

(FOR INFORMATION ABOUT the Discovering Diversity Profile which measures your development within these cornerstones contact info@Lenora-BillingsHarris.com.) Each dimension requires personal action. However, they can be approached in any order.

The first Cornerstone of Diversity is knowledge. The diversity collisions that occur in the workplace are often accidental, unintended statements that are offensive or inappropriate. When knowledge is lacking, people will rely on the stereotypical or biased information gathered throughout a lifetime. Knowledge, in this context, is *the extent to which an individual possesses information about others from diverse backgrounds and cultures.* The more factual data that you have about other cultures and groups, the easier it is to be comfortable when interacting with people different than you.

Use resources from films and videos, books, magazines, and the Internet (library, chat rooms, etc.) and talk to people within the group. Gathering information from these resources impacts our views and actions in relationship to people different than ourselves. The more accurate information we have about others, the more likely it is we will develop accurate opinions, feelings, and behaviors. Remember that you are only getting the perspective of that author, that director, that person, so it is important to use many different sources of information. The following is a list of possible resources for you.

Places and Events:

    Ethnic museums and memorials

    Historical societies

    Ethnic cooking classes

    Language classes

    Ethnic studies at colleges, universities, and libraries

    Different places of worship (mosques, synagogues, churches of different denominations, etc.)

    Fine arts events

    Community theater

    Resources from government agencies (Human Rights Commission, Women's Commission, Equal Opportunity Offices, etc.)

    Engage in social networks online with people you don't normally associate with. Follow people of a different ethnicity, political view, or generation on Facebook and Twitter.

Films Key:

> G= gender
> D = disability
> R = racism
> S = sexual orientation
> V = valuing and respecting differences in general
> C = culture
> A = age

A Beautiful Mind (2001) (D) This film is about math prodigy who is able to solve problems baffled the greatest of minds, and how he overcame years of suffering through schizophrenia to win the Nobel Prize.

A Day Without A Mexican (2004) (C/R) California wakes up one morning to discover Mexicans, over a third of the population, have suddenly disappeared. The economy and day to day life screech to a halt as the cast tries to discover where the Latinos have gone.

A League of Their Own (1992) (G) Two sisters join the first female professional baseball league and struggle to help it succeed amidst their own growing rivalry.

ABCD (1999) (C) With a mix of humor and poignancy, the film presents a compelling look at the emotional consequences of growing up without a firm cultural identity.

Albert Nobbs (2011) (G/S) A woman in 19th century Ireland is forced to work and live as a man in order to earn a living. She befriends another woman posing as a man and learns about the woman's wife, a type of relationship she too hopes to have one day.

Akeelah and the Bee (2006) (C) An 11-year old girl from South Los Angeles lives in an environment that threatens to strangle her aspirations of being a National Spelling Bee Champion.

American History X (1998) (R) A neo-Nazi skinhead tries to prevent his younger brother from going down the same wrong path that he did. This film explores the harsh reality of how people learn to hate and how challenging it can be to unlearn that type of brainwashing.

Amistad (1997) (R) Based on a true story, this movie navigates through the historical tale of an enslaved Africans uprising on the ship La Amistad. The narrative brings the watcher through the uprising followed by the subsequent imprisonment and court battle in the United States.

Antonia's Line (1995) (C) A Belgian matron establishes and, for several generations, oversees a close-knit, matriarchal community where feminism and liberalism thrive.

Anytown, USA (2006) (D) This documentary is about the race for mayor in a small New Jersey town- a race fought between a legally blind, tough-talking Republican; an old guard Democrat looking to make comeback; and a legally blind, independent write-in candidate.

A Patch of Blue (1965) (D/R) An educated black man becomes friends with a blind underprivileged girl. Their relationship grows despite their racially divided community as he begins to teach her how to navigate their world.

Atanarjuat: The Fast Runner (2001) (C) A remarkable film that dramatizes an Inuit legend with Inuit actors, in Inuktitut with English subtitles. This film gives an authentic narrative of a culture in her traditional lands.

A Time to Kill (1996) (R) Two white racists rape and attempt to kill a ten year old girl. Her father, fearing that they will not be prosecuted, kills both men. This is the story of the man, a young lawyer, and the trial that he must face for the murders.

Avalon (1990) (C) A Russian family comes to the USA at the beginning of the Twentieth Century. There, the family and their children try to make themselves a better future in the so-called 'promised land.'

Babe (1995) (V) Babe, a pig, is raised on a farm by a mother sheepdog. He faces the heartbreaking realities of the intended fate of farm animals while proving himself useful as farm help with what skills he has learned from the dog that reared him.

Beauty and the Beast (1991) (V) This classic story brings two people together through love despite differences and a physical deformity that does not match original expectations.

Before Night Falls (2000) (C) An evocative and moving story based on the life of Cuban writer, Reinaldo Arenas.

Bend it like Beckham (2002) (C) In this tale of a search for identity Jess Bharma, a teenage girl, walks away from her orthodox Sikh traditions in order to play with a soccer team in another country.

Beshkempir: The Adopted Son (1998) (A/C) In a Kyrgyz village, five older women adopt an infant foundling. Jump ahead about 12 years: the boy, Beshkempir, is entering puberty, the age, his granny says, when life goes berserk.

Billy Elliot (2000) (G/V) Billy Elliot defies convention and the wishes of his father when he is drawn into ballet as a child. He struggles to hide and continue with his ballet lessons and follow his passion.

Birth of a Nation (1915) (R) This controversial silent film includes actors in black face paint that portray African American men in an unfavorable light. Due to the high levels of racism presented, it faced public outcry and viewing was banned in some locations.

Bloody Sunday (2002) (R) A documentary-style drama showing the events that lead up to the tragic incident on January 30, 1972 in the Northern Ireland town of Derry when a protest march led by civil rights activist Ivan Cooper was fired up by British troops, killing 13 protesters and wounding 14 more.

Boy's Don't Cry (1999) (G) The story of the life of Brandon Teena, a transgender teen who preferred life in a male identity until it was discovered he was born biologically female

Boys on the Side (1995) (S) This motion picture is about three women, on the road, reaching understanding, respect and care for one another. The trio is very diverse in the way that one woman is a lesbian, another suffering with AIDS, and the other seeking one-night stands and a good man.

Boyz 'N the Hood (1991) (C) Tré Styles' story begins as a child when he gets in trouble and is sent to live with his father in order to learn life lessons. We follow him and his friends as they grow up in Crenshaw, a notorious Los Angeles ghetto.

Brokeback Mountain (2005) (S) Based on the E. Annie Proulx story about a forbidden and secretive relationship between two cowboys and their lives over the years.

Crash (2004) (R) This film takes a challenging and thought- provoking look at the complexities of racial tolerance in contemporary America. CRASH boldly reminds us of the importance of tolerance as it ventures beyond color lines….and uncovers the truth of our shared humanity.

Dances With Wolves (1990) (C) Lieutenant Dunbar comes to know a local tribe while he is working on the western frontier. He grows to embrace and live the native culture as he seeks a place within it.

David and Lisa (1962) (D) The film's main characters meet while in treatment, Lisa for dissociate identity disorder and David for obsessive compulsive disorder. They grow and learn to understand each other in this small independent film.

Do the Right Thing (1989) (R) On the hottest day of summer, racial tensions rise in the Bedford-Stuyvesant section of Brooklyn. Community members move against local Korean and Italian business owners with tragedy resulting.

Dorian Blues (2004) (S) A refreshing and witty coming-of-age comedy about a small-town man who is homosexual.

Edge of America (2003) (C) Based on a true story, a black educator takes a job teaching high school English at the Three Nations Reservation, and is coaxed into coaching the girls' basketball team. This film does a good job of avoiding the misrepresentation in the media about Native Americans and their culture by presenting a realistic portrayal of Indian life in America today.

Erin Brockovich (2000) (V) An unemployed single mother becomes a legal assistant and almost single-handedly brings down a California power company accused of polluting a city's water supply.

Far from Heaven (2002) (R) In 1950s Connecticut, a housewife faces a marital crisis and mounting racial tension in the outside world.

Frida (2002) (D) A biography of artist Frida Kahlo, who channeled the pain of a crippling injury and tempestuous marriage into her work.

Fried Green Tomatoes (1991) (G) In this movie version of Friend Green Tomatoes the relationship between Ruth and Idgie is downplayed, although it still won an award from the Gay & Lesbian Alliance Against Defamation for best feature film with lesbian content. The story follows the relationship and lives of the women as Ruth marries Frank Bennett and enters an abusive relationship.

Gandhi (1982) (R) This biography of Mahatma Ganhi starts when he is 24 years old and is removed from a train's first class section due to his Indian heritage and despite the fact that he had the proper fare. It continues on to portray Gandhi's struggle for people's rights and freedom in Africa and India.

Genghis Blues (1999) (D) This is a fascinating documentary about Paul Pena, a blind blues guitarist who heard Tuvan musicians on his radio and then made a brave step into the unknown by setting out to find them. Cultures collide in style as the Tuvans and the San Franciscan get tuned up and create some mean throat-singing blues.

Get Real (1998) (S) A coming-of-age and coming-out story about two boys in a British high school.

Ghosts of Mississippi (1996) (R) Based on the true story of Mrs. Medger Evers, widowed when her civil rights leader husband was murdered, fights along with a district attorney to seek justice and conviction of the murderer.

Girl, Interrupted (1999) (D) Based on writer Susanna Kaysen's account of her 18-month stay at a mental hospital in the 1960s.

Glory (1989) (C/R) Robert Gould Shaw becomes the leader of the first Black volunteer company during the United States Civil War. He faces danger in fighting both the Confederates as well as prejudice within the Union army.

Glory Road (2006) (C) The true story of the team that changed college basketball. Coach Don Haskins simply started the best players he could find- history's first all-African American lineup.

Good Night, and Good Luck (2005) (C) This film gives us a glimpse into the 1950s when the threat of Communism created an air of paranoia in the United States. Edward R. Murrow and his producer Fred W. Friendly stand by their convictions and helped to bring down one of the most controversial senators in American history.

Hiroshima Maiden (1988) (R) The atomic bomb dropping on Hiroshima in 1945 resulted in a group of Japanese women with serious disfigurements. We follow one of them, Miyeko, as she comes to the United States for plastic surgery and struggles against the hatred she discovers here.

Hotel Rwanda (2004) (R) This film is the true life story of Paul Rusesabagina, a hotel manager who housed over a thousand Tutsis refugees during their struggle against the Hutu militia in Rwanda.

I am Sam (2001) (V) A mentally-challenged man fights for custody of his 7-year old daughter and, in the process, teaches his cold-hearted lawyer the value of love and family.

In America (2003) (C) An Irish immigrant family adjusts to life in the United States.

In the Heat of the Night (1967) (R) The story starts when Virgil Tibbs, an African-American detective is arrested at a train station. The local police chief soon releases Virgil only to put him in an odd predicament by asking for his assistance in solving a murder in the racist southern town of Sparta.

Machuca (2004) (C) Two boys from very opposite socio-economic backgrounds observe a political coup in their native Chile.

Malcolm X (1992) (R) This biography covers some of the key points of Malcolm X's life story. It starts in his childhood, highlights racism he observed, and moves on towards his work and experiences as an adult including his incarceration, conversion to Islam, and assassination.

Mississippi Burning (1988) (R) The murder of a civil rights worker is investigated by two FBI agents with contrasting styles. They seek to find the truth in a tight lipped and segregated community.

Monsoon Wedding (2001) (C) A traditional arranged marriage in India brings together culture and chaos as families struggle to resolve issues from their lives including abuse and infidelity.

Munich (2005) (C) This historical film covers the covert actions of the Israeli government as it retaliates with murder in response to the massacre of Israeli athletes during the 1972 Munich Summer Olympics.

My Left Foot (1989) (D) Christy Brown, a spastic quadriplegic due to cerebral palsy, defies the odds and everyone's expectations as he learns to both paint and write with his one working limb. He grows to become an excellent writer.

North Country (2005) (G) An unforgiving look at the treatment of female workers at a male-dominated Minnesota mine. This film takes a look at the struggle of one female worker that endures daily torment, yet is the only one that refuses to back down from making the mine accountable.

Osama (2003) (C/G) A 12-year old Afghan girl's mother loses her job when the Taliban stops funding for the hospital where she works. The girl disguises herself as a boy in order to support her family under the repressive regime. Inspired by a true story, Osama is the first entirely Afghan film shot since the fall of the Taliban.

Patch Adams (1998) (V) Patch Adams is a medical doctor that goes against convention by treating his patients with humor. While his colleagues do not understand his work, those that he actually treats appreciate it greatly.

Philadelphia (1993) (S) An attorney with AIDS is fired from his job when one of his colleagues notices physical symptoms of his condition. He fights back along with an unlikely small town and homophobic lawyer who happens to be the only one willing to represent him.

Pocahontas (1995) (C) This Disney film is based on the history and folklore surrounding a Native American woman. The story itself is a fictionalized version of her introduction to an Englishman named John Smith.

Rabbit Proof Fence (2002) (R) In 1931, three aboriginal girls escape after being plucked from their homes to be trained as domestic staff and set off on a trek across the Outback.

Radio (2003) (D) The true life story of a high school coach who takes a developmentally challenged man under his wings thereby changing his life, and the lives of just about everyone in the South Carolina town in which they live.

Rang De Basanti (2006) (C/R) A young English film maker recruits students from Delhi University to act in her docu-drama about Indian revolutionaries Bhagat Sing, Chandrashekhar Azad and their contemporaries and their fight for freedom from the British Raj.

Red Tails (2012) (R/D) A crew of African American pilots in the Tuskegee training program, are called into duty under the guidance of Col. A.J. Bullard. The WWII film looks at the cultural clashes betwee Blacks and Whites in the segregated military.

Rainman (1988) (D) A story where the selfish Charlie Babitt is left only a small sum by his rich father. The father passes on his fortune to Charlie's autistic brother Raymond. Charlie kidnaps Raymond to try and get the fortune, but gradually develops a genuine fondness for his savant brother.

Real Women Have Curves (2002) (C) Teenage Mexican-American Ana earns a college scholarship, but comes under pressure from her parents to work for the family, rather than continue her education. Ana spends the summer in a sewing factory and learns to respect the employees' hard work and values, but eventually realizes her heart lies in a college education.

Remember the Titans (2000) (R) Based on the true story of a newly appointed African-American coach and his high school team on their first season as a racially integrated unit.

Roots (1977) (R/C) A mix of family, cultural and social history. It tells the story of a man kidnapped from Africa to become a slave, the marriage to his wife and the tale of their daughter. His daughter's husband eventually earns them their freedom. The film takes a look at the prejudices and social conventions of the world of slavery and the gradual changes in attitudes.

Save the Last Dance (2001) (C) Sarah has her dreams of becoming a ballerina cut short when her mother dies and she moves in with her father, who lives in a predominately African American area of Chicago. Sarah has to deal with life in a new school where she is one of the few white students there. She makes friends with one of the students and falls in love with his brother, where she confronts people's reactions to their relationship.

Schindler's List (1993) (R) Steven Spielberg produced this award winning biography of the German Oskar Schindler, man who turned his factory into a refugee for Jews under threat from the Nazi regime. He

saved the lives of more than one thousand people through his actions
and bravery.

Seabiscuit (2003) (V) The true story of the undersized Depression-
era racehorse whose victories lifted not only the spirits of the team behind it but also those of the nation as well.

Secret Ballot "Raye Makhfi" (2001) (C) This film vividly demonstrates the physical, logistical, psychological, political and social challenges of bringing some semblance of democracy to other cultures, let
alone the Middle East.

Shrek (2001) (V) Ogre Shrek discovers the value of true love and
teamwork with a wide range of characters in this animated film. He wins
over the hearts of his community and they move past their assumption
that ogres must be murderous creatures.

Smoke Signals (1998) (C) This film is billed as the first feature
written, directed, co-produced and acted by American Indians. "Smoke
Signals" is a journey of the heart, an exploration of what it means to be
Indian, venturing into the world outside the reservation.

Snow White (1987) (V) This is the live action version of the classic Disney animation, a tale in which characters are perceived and valued (often wrongly in the case of the dwarfs) according to their meeting
physical beauty standards.

Sophie's Choice (1982) (C/R) Holocaust survivor Sophie is involved
in a relationship with Nathan, a Jewish man, who has a Holocaust obses-
sion. While Nathan's moods become increasingly depressing and violent,
Sophie meets writer Stingo, who falls for her. Sophie has to deal with her
past, the loss of one of her children, and the choice as to who she should
be with.

Something New (2006) (C/R) An intelligent romantic comedy that
chooses to deal with issues of race and perception in a straight-forward
way, from a point of view not often seen: that of a successful, upper- class
African-American woman.

Something the Lord Made (2004) (V) A dramatization of the relationship between heart surgery pioneers that changed the face of
medicine.

Sometimes in April (2005) (R) A chilling drama framed by the
Rwandan genocide.

Spanglish (2004) (C) An upscale Chef and his wife hire a Mexican housekeeper with limited command of English as their help for the
summer. In this comedy, she has to contend with the language barrier, the

eccentric way of life of the family, and how the wife treats the housekeeper's daughter almost like one of her own.

Syriana (C) Tracks several disparate characters across the globe as their lives are impacted by ruthless competition for power of wealth that drives the energy industry.

The Color Purple (1985) (R/C) This tells the story of Celie who must deal with the realities of growing up as an African American woman in the South in the 1930s. After suffering abuse by her father she gradually finds herself worth through friendship and romance in the face of racism.

The Diary of Anne Frank (1959) V/C The movie was based on the actual personal diary of Anne Frank, a Jewish girl who lived in a hiding place with her family during World War II. The diary was published after the end of the war by her father Otto. By this time all his other family members were killed by the Nazis.

The Gods Must Be Crazy (1980) (C/V) A story of how a tribe in the African desert, previously happy, have their lives turned upside down by a Coca-Cola bottle which has been carelessly thrown away. This leads one of the tribe members, Xi, to encounter Western culture for the first time with the eyes of an outsider.

The Hiding Place (1975) (R) Two Dutch sisters are sent to a Nazi concentration camp as punishment for trying to hide Jews from transportation to their deaths. One sister dies, while the other is released as her Christian faith is tested to the limit by the suffering she undergoes.

The Hours (2002) (A/G) The story of how the novel "Mrs. Dalloway" affects three generations of women, all of whom, in one way or another, have to deal with suicide in their lives.

The Joy Luck Club (1993) (C) This is an exploration of the lives of four Chinese women, living in the United States, and their relationships with their first generation Chinese-American daughters. The film looks at the social and cultural tensions between mother and child as they discuss their lives over games of mahjong.

The Pianist (2002) (C/R) A polish Jewish musician struggles to survive the destruction of the Warsaw ghetto of World War II.

The Snow Walker (2003) (C) A pilot who delivers supplies to tribes in the backwoods of the Canadian north is implored to escort a sick young Inuit woman to a hospital. On the flight back he crashes the plane and he has to learn with Kanaalaq how to survive in the cold region, forming a bond of respect and friendship with her.

Thumbelina (1994) (V) A fairy-tale of an elderly woman who longs for a daughter to love and thanks to a witch, has a tiny daughter who can fit in a matchbox. Thumbelina worries no one will love her because of her tiny size, but she is found by the Prince of the Fairies, who finds her enchanting.

To Kill a Mockingbird (1962) (R/D) Set in the 1930's, this is the story of attorney Atticus Finch who takes on the defense of an African-American man accused of rape. Despite his efforts to show the inconsistencies in the evidence his client is convicted and eventually lynched, leading Atticus' family to become aware of the injustices in society.

Transamerica (2005) (G) A pre-operative male-to-female transsexual takes an unexpected journey when she learns that she fathered a son, now a teenage runaway hustling on the streets of New York.

Water (2005) (G) Set in the 1930s during the rise of the independence struggles against British colonial rule, this film examines the plight of a group of widows forced into poverty at a temple in the holy city of Varanasi. It focuses on the relationship between one of the widows, who wants to escape the social restrictions imposed on widows, and a man who is from a lower caste and a follower of Mahatma Gandhi.

West Side Story (1961) (C/R) A musical inspired by Romeo and Juliet where lovers from opposing white and Puerto Rican New York gangs plan to run away, as the two gangs prepare for a major war for control of the streets. The lovers intervene to try and stop the violence, but with tragic results.

Whale Rider (2002) (C) A contemporary story of love, rejection and triumph as one young Maori girl dares to confront the past, change the present and determine the future in the ways of the Ancients.

Why We Fight (2006) (C) This documentary examines why war headlines reign strong across our nightly newscasts by looking back at more than 50 years of fighting.

Wizard of Oz (1939) (V) This classic story brings together a group with seemingly insurmountable differences; a lion, a tin man, a scarecrow, and a young girl. They prove they have the qualities they think they lack and as a team they prepare to confront an evil witch.

Young Frankenstein (1974) (V) In this comedy young Frankenstein's creation escapes after being captured by frightened townsfolk and eventually Frankenstein works to give him more brain power. He is then able to reason with the townsfolk that he should be allowed to live a normal life.

General:

Public television programs such as Front Line

The Internet (directories, libraries, chat rooms, bulletin boards, etc.)

Magazines:

Black Enterprise

Diverse in Higher Education

DiveristyInc Magazine

Diversity Woman

Ebony

AARP Magazine

Essence

The Advocate

10

Latino

Large Woman

Working Woman

Woman's World

Books:

See Bibliography and Reference List at the end of this book

Making a Difference

1. Review a movie about a group with whom you are reasonably unfamiliar. As you view it, notice the differences and similarities as compared to your own culture. Note how the movie impacted your feelings. What, if anything, might you do differently as a result of viewing the film? Focus particularly on similarities and differences of:

   non-verbal messages
   gender
   ethnicity and race
   age
   religious issues and beliefs
   physical and mental abilities
   how respect is shown to authority
   communication styles
   concepts such as personal space, time, family, education
   foods
   traditions and rituals

2. Identify a group with whom you know you have a negative bias or attitude.
3. Read a book or magazine about the group with the express purpose of identifying things they have in common with you.
4. List in the space below the specific things you learned.

Articles and Webinars
http://goo.gl/U3fTPO
http://goo.gl/7ZwdeL

CHAPTER 6

SOME STEREOTYPES *are* TRUE, AREN'T THEY?

> *When Hitler attacked the Jews, I was not a*
> *Jew, therefore I was not concerned.*
> *When Hitler attacked the Catholics, I was not*
> *a Catholic, and therefore, I was not concerned.*
> *When Hitler attacked the unions and the in-*
> *dustrialists, I was not a member of the unions*
> *and I was not concerned.*
> *Then Hitler attacked me and the Protestant*
> *church -- and there was nobody left to be con-*
> *cerned.*
>
> — Pastor Martin Niemoller

A STEREOTYPE IS A GENeralized statement applied to everyone in the group, as though the entire group is the same. Any belief or characteristic, applied to an entire group, immediately makes it invalid because no characteristics are held by everyone in the group.

Stereotypical beliefs sometimes come from some degree of truth, however. There is probably someone in the group who fits the stereotype. The challenge is to acknowledge people as individuals without generalizing that individual's behaviors or characteristics.

For example, a stereotype about African Americans is "Black people have rhythm." It is true that many African Americans are rhythmic. However, all African Americans do not have rhythm, and many people of other cultures do. Another stereotype is depicted in the movie, *White Men Can't Jump.*

The title poked fun at the stereotype about White men as though none of them could play basketball. Viewers of this movie have the opportunity to see that White men can, in fact, jump.

There is no such thing as a "good" stereotype. All stereotypical beliefs lead to inaccurate assumptions about individuals, whether the belief is a positive one or not. In the United States, there is a widely held belief that

Asian children are smart, especially in mathematics and science. It is true that many Asian American children test well in these subjects. However, they are not born smarter than other people. Their ability, as it relates to these two subjects, is a result of their environment.

All Asian Americans are not highly intelligent or skilled in these areas, especially if they are sixth or seventh generation Asian, and do not speak the language of their ancestors, although many have grown up in a home environment that strongly supports education. In Malcolm Gladwell's book, *Outliers* there is a reasonable explanation for this phenomenon that has to do with linguistics and math. (See *Outliers*, chapter 8.)

Here is an example of how even a *"good"* stereotype can be damaging:

Imagine you are observing a third-grade class. The class is composed of White children except for three. One male child is a Latino. Another male child is an African American, and the third child of difference is a Chinese American female.

This teacher is someone your parents are delighted to have in the school system. He is the type of individual that goes out of his way to help his students excel. He truly loves each child, spends his own money for additional resources, stays after school, and comes in early to be available to assist students in any way he can. In other words, his intentions are good. However, he is not aware of his own stereotypes. Therefore, he is not aware of how those stereotypes impact his behavior.

It's September, thus he does not yet know his students individually very well. As he plans his lesson, the teacher begins to determine which students he may need to spend additional time with in order that they too can perform well. He's going to teach long division. Which students do you think he will most likely conclude need additional assistance?

The next day he goes into class, teaches long division, and then distributes math problems to each student. He immediately walks over to the African American boy. Now, remember, his intentions are good. He wants to help. Is it possible the African American male is doing well?

Of course, yes, it is possible. Is it likely that this young student will, in some way, let the teacher know that he does not need help? That behavior is most unlikely. The teacher then walks over to the Latino student. Is it possible he too needs no assistance? It is unlikely that he will tell the teacher he does not need help.

The teacher never walks over to the Chinese American girl, even though another stereotype in the United States is girls do not perform as well as boys in math and science. In this case the ethnic stereotype is stronger than the gender stereotype. Is it possible that the Chinese American girl does need help? Of course, the answer is yes. Is it likely she will ask for help? Most likely, no. Even at eight years old, in the third grade, she probably knows from messages around her, in comic strips, from adults, and from peers, that she is supposed to be a good math student. Additionally, she may have learned from her culture never to ask a person in authority a question in public. This would imply that the person in authority was not clear, and could cause the authority figure to possibly "lose face."

Which student(s) has the teacher's behavior impacted? I hope you would agree that all of the students have been negatively impacted. Certainly there would be some White children who do need help. The teacher neglected them, while the African American and the Latino received unnecessary attention, which could have sent the wrong message to the other students.

As the children go to the playground, the teacher's behavior could now impact their behavior toward each other. Some students might assume that the Latino and the African American are teacher's pets and start a fight with them. Other students might assume that the Latino and African American must be slow learners because they get so much attention, and start a fight with them.

If they continue to see the same or similar messages acted out, that teacher's behavior could impact students behavior later in life, when working with people who are different than they are ethnically. Our newspapers are replete with stories about bullies in school and in the workplace. It is impossible to get rid of stereotypes entirely. The best we can do is become more aware of our own stereotypes. This way we can become more aware of how our stereotypes impact our behavior.

Becoming aware of stereotypes includes listening to that inner/ego voice that quotes generalized statements, and then choosing not to act on those stereotypical beliefs. It takes a conscious effort to ignore them or explore them to learn the facts.

Making a Difference

Watch a television program or a movie with a friend, with the specific intention of identifying all of the stereotypical behaviors and statements depicted in the show. Discuss which biases and stereotypes you both observed and which ones you have believed and accepted for a long time.

Ask someone you trust to alert you (in private) anytime you make a stereotypical comment. It is only with this feedback that you can become more aware of how often you may rely on your own stereotypes. Record what you have learned.

When you recognize that you are having a communications conflict with someone, identify the many ways that person may be different from you.

Perhaps their communication style is different. Perhaps their values, faith, beliefs, or politics are different. Or perhaps there are visible differences such as gender, ethnicity, or age. Set an objective to evaluate the specific interaction between yourself and that person. In other words, evaluate the facts instead of relying on stereotypes. Then discuss your findings with the individual in order to resolve the conflict.

Article
Seven Inclusion Acts of Engagement
http://goo.gl/9oW3OM

Chapter 7

How Do I Begin *to* Improve My Understanding *of* People Different Than Me?

I use not only all of the brains I have, but all I can borrow.

— Woodrow Wilson

UNDERSTANDING IS "THE extent to which an individual comprehends how others feel and why they behave as they do," according to Tolbert, Mendez-Russell, and Wilderson, the authors of the *Discovering Diversity Profile.* With enhanced awareness we begin to see how our personal reality may not be the only reality. Better awareness helps us understand how others feel. It clarifies who we are in comparison to others, and it gives us a basis for contrasting our own cultural viewpoints with those of other people.

Because of cultural differences, people often see the same situation differently. For instance, among the Navajo Nation there is no a direct way to say, "be on time," because time is relative. Things happen "when it is time." If you are doing something important with other people, being on time is not considered to be more important. In the mainstream "western" business world, "time is money." Being on time, being punctual is very important, regardless of what you may be doing with others beforehand.

During one of my seminars with an Arizona client, a participant explained how difficult it sometimes is to impart the significance of being on time when his group is working with some of the Native Americans on the reservation. This is not an example of right or wrong. This is an example of being different. He said there was a trainee who did not return to class for three days, and also did not call to explain the absence. When the student finally did return, his reason for being absent was that he had had a death in the family and had ceremonies to attend. Of course, this was much more important than going to class. Time is relative.

With an enhanced understanding of why people do what they do, we can become less quick to judge and more able to empathize. Empathy is the ability to make connections with others on an emotional level.

People who are empathic and aware can comprehend the emotions others are experiencing. They tend to recognize the reasons for points of view held by people from diverse backgrounds. This goes beyond knowledge of facts.

There are many resources around you, right in your community, that can help enhance understanding and enable you to develop more empathy for diverse groups. The key is to explore many sources and, most important, to talk to people within the group about which you want to learn. As you talk to people, realize that they may not know all of the answers to your questions.

When you grow up within a culture and practice its traditions, you may not necessarily know why the traditions are as they are.

While attending a National Speakers Association Convention, I decided to attend a Jewish worship service for the first time. I was so excited to have the opportunity. Having been raised a Baptist, I was curious about the traditions of the Jewish faith.

I quickly discovered that my friends, who were sitting next to me and who are Jewish, did not necessarily know why we were performing some of the wonderful rituals that were included in the service. In contrast, many Christians practice traditions such as having an evergreen Christmas tree, lights on the tree, and giving gifts, yet they do not know why each of those traditions has become part of their religion. In fact, some of the traditions that are thought to be religious are actually secular.

As you plan your study, include religion, language, foods, music, and the arts. If you study or participate in any of these areas of focus, you will develop a better appreciation for and under standing of diverse groups.

After 9/11, Muslims throughout the United States were targeted with violence and racism because of the actions of radical militants. The effects of the devastating attack on the US continues to this day and tensions seem to continue to mount between Muslims and non-Muslims. Before you jump to judgment, take time to learn some of the actual tenets of Islam, instead of relying on hearsay. We fear that which we do not understand. Learn the difference between cultural choices versus religious rules regarding the wearing of the burquaa and hijab.

Religion establishes many of the values of a culture. Language demonstrates the values and biases of various cultural groups. For instance, "white lie" versus a "lie." As a result of institutionalized racism, many synonyms using the word white are good, and synonyms with the black mean something bad. Ethnic food helps explain the behavior of a culture. You need to do more than just eat and enjoy the food, but it is a key to cultural context . You need to research why certain foods have become staples for that particular ethnic group.

I discovered that my favorite vegetable, collard greens, which is considered "soul food," has a story connected to it. During the early days of slave labor, the plantation masters did not provide very much food for their enslaved Africans. Therefore, the African women searched through the undeveloped parts of the plantation—the woods and the forest—to see what might be growing that they recognized from Africa. They soon discovered that collard greens, salad greens, and other green leafy vegetables were growing wild on many of the Southern plantations. Since the plantation owners did not eat these foods, the enslaved Africans were able to expand the amount of healthy food available to them.

All ethnic food has a story connected to it, which can help you understand that culture a bit better.

The following is a list of places, events, activities and resources that might be available in your local area. The more you travel around the country and outside of the country the more you will expand your personal cultural competencies.

Ethnic museums and memorials

Historic societies

Ethnic cooking classes

Language classes

Ethnic studies at colleges, universities, and libraries, such as Asian American studies, African American studies, women's studies, and so on.

Various places of worship, such as mosques, synagogues, churches of different denominations, the Bahai faith center, temples

Pow Wows

Fine arts events

Women's shelters

Homeless shelters

Special Olympics

Anytown, USA (1-800-283-Hugs)

The Hispanic Women's Conference

100 Black Women Clubs

Oktoberfest

Greek festivals
Ethnic restaurants
Rodeos
Community theater
The Human Rights Commission
The Women's Commission
The Internet offers a vast resource of culturally diverse discussion
     boards, and more

Making a Difference

     Set a time and date to volunteer or visit one of the suggest-
ed resources. Make it a fun event. Go with friends, relatives, or
your children and discuss what you hope to learn. As you participate, notice what customs are different from your own. Plan
a debriefing discussion with your friends to compare notes and
observations.

**Webinar: PC or Not PC: 5 Diversity
Myths Debunked
http://goo.gl/59tpVh**

CHAPTER 8

IF I ACCEPT *the* BELIEFS *and* BEHAVIORS *of* SOME PEOPLE, DOES THAT MEAN I CONDONE THEM?

> *A perfectly normal person is rare in our civilization.*
>
> — Karen Horney

THE IMMEDIATE ANSWER to this question is, No. To condone means to approve. Acceptance the way I use it, as it relates to accepting others different than you, means *having the willingness and ability to respect and value characteristics, customs, and behaviors of others.* This does not include inappropriate behavior, such as breaking the law or harassing others. With acceptance we can become more relaxed and open minded with others.

By developing the ability to accept others, ultimately respect for each individual is established. Seeing value in having a diversity of viewpoints, even if they cause a debate, is healthy and productive. The outcome can be a broadening of understanding for all parties, even if they agree to disagree. Think of your own family. Does everyone agree all the time? Probably not, but hopefully everyone still accepts each other. In the workplace, the strongest, most effective teams have a diversity of viewpoints from many different types of people. The decisions made by such a team then reflect the group's best thinking, instead of just the ideas of the most powerful member.

Acceptance manifests itself through our behavior in many ways. This story illustrates the point. When I lived in Arizona, my husband and I socialized with two other couples frequently. The six of us often went to dinner together, and we did not always sit next to our life partner. One evening at Ayako's, a fun Japanese restaurant, we experienced a lack of acceptance. The couple combinations were as follows: one White couple, one African American couple, and one Bi-racial couple. Another couple, Pete and Diane, who were strangers to us, and who happened to be White were seated at our table to enjoy the chef's entertaining meal preparation. Since we were planning to have great fun, we greeted the new couple immediately, with the hopes that they would be comfortable talking to and responding to the chef, as we intended to do.

As the evening wore on it became obvious, due to their questions of us, that they were trying desperately to determine who was married to whom, and why we were all together. To Diane and Pete the "ethnicity matchup" did not fit. There were two White women and one African American woman; two African American men and one White man. Since we were not sitting next to our mates, and only one couple wore wedding bands, this was puzzling Pete and Diane. They never asked directly who was with whom, but it was obvious that they were wondering.

Pete asked, "How did you become friends?" One of the guys responded, "We have just known each other a long time, and like to party together." As the meal ended, and all of us were

leaving the restaurant, Diane said to me, "I got it! You all sell Amway, and you are in town for a rally!" Isn't it sad that she could not accept that we were friends *just because* and not because of anything in particular. When Pe0te saw us pair up finally, he seemed relieved to see that only one couple was Bi-racial.

When we are not willing to accept diversity as being normal, we look for all kinds of rationales.

Making a Difference

Developing acceptance requires you to "get out of your comfort zone." Broaden your viewpoint by trying the following suggestions:
1. Seek different points of view from friends and associates by discussing politics, religion, creationism versus evolution, right to life versus pro-choice, etc. Remember, it is okay to agree to disagree.
2. Listen to children. Really listen. When adults do not intervene, often children show a refreshing point of view on many things.

3. Become a volunteer for Big Brother/Big Sister in your community or another similar organization. In addition to being a role model for your little "sister" or "brother," you will learn many things about a real person who has a background different from yours.

4. If you are a sales or customer service representative, intentionally sell to or serve a customer who represents a
     group you tend to be intolerant of or impatient with. Focus on being patient and asking questions for clarity.

5. Be aware of your stereotypes, but do not act on them.

6. Keep a journal or diary of your experiences.

7. As you explore and practice the suggestions listed in this section of each chapter, you will be developing the fourth cornerstone of diversity, "behavior."

Articles and Webinars
http://goo.gl/U3fTPO
http://goo.gl/7ZwdeL

CHAPTER 9

I Realize Leveraging Diversity May Be *the* Right Thing *to* Do, *but* What's *the* Business Need?

*We must learn to live together as brothers or
we are going to perish together as fools.*

— Rev. Dr. Martin Luther King, Jr.

Before embarking on any diversity initiative, including Diversity Awareness Training, your organization should be clear about its purpose for doing so and the results it expects. The clients with whom I have worked generally embark upon diversity and inclusion work for one of three reasons:

1) In their leadership's mind, it is the right thing to do.
2) To avoid costly lawsuits.
3) To enhance organizational productivity and profitability.

It's the right thing to do

Several years ago, the American Heart Association decided to embrace diversity at all levels. As a nonprofit organization that provides services to the public, their leadership realized that heart attacks do not discriminate. Therefore, their staff and volunteers needed to develop a fuller understanding of all potential clientele.

The American Heart Association's Diversity Initiative had several segments. We offered diversity/cultural competence training to their community outreach volunteers across the country; they analyzed their marketing materials to make them more inclusive; and we evaluated recruiting tactics to discover more and better ways to recruit volunteers from all ethnic groups and economic levels.

A health services provider recognized that its Board of Directors, in its makeup, did not reflect the communities the organization serves. The initiative started at the board level and then reached all employees within every clinic and its central offices.

Although both organizations embarked upon diversity because they believed it was the right thing to do, they both quickly recognized the bottom-line impact even though they are non-profits. With a higher focus on valuing differences, organizations are able to more easily recognize how they may have overlooked simple procedures that inhibit or prohibit prospective clients from utilizing their services. Clinic hours of operation and location sometimes prohibited American Indians living on a reservation from utilizing services. The board and staff had, in the past, wondered why their utilization numbers from American Indians were so low. Once they recognized this problem, they were able to change clinic hours and arranged to provide transportation for individuals needing consultations and health checkups.

More and more companies are turning to diversity initiatives for a number of reasons, As a result, they are discovering that the effect of being a diverse workplace boosts their bottom line as well as the perception of the company from the consumer public.

From these examples you can quickly see that "doing the right thing" can lead to higher utilization of services, efficiency, as well as other good business outcomes.

To avoid lawsuits and discrimination claims

Although this motivation is negative and reactive rather than proactive, many diversity awareness classes have been conducted because organizations have suffered the consequences of insensitivity and/or direct discrimination. In November of 1996, Texaco settled a discrimination case out of court for over $17 million. In 2010, Kmart agreed to pay $120,000 in an age discrimination suit. Wal-Mart has been under fire for sex discrimination, though a major class action lawsuit was dismissed recently. There is no doubt that multiple class actions suits will be filed in the future. No matter how large or small the company, paying money for inappropriate behavior in the workplace is a drain to the bottom line. It damages the public image. It affects recruiting, retention, and productivity among all employees.

While many organizations have jumped on the "diversity bandwagon," many have only chosen to provide diversity training. This has been a mistake. With only training and no plans to truly evaluate systems and processes, to be sure all individuals are respected, developed, and encouraged to reach their highest potential, frequently more misunderstandings erupt instead of fewer.

The courts are becoming inundated with discrimination cases as a result of more awareness from the public about these actions. Regardless of the outcome, all individuals should have the right to work in an environment that supports them as contributing employees, regardless of their gender, sexual orientation or identity, or ethnicity. When I share information about various court cases or pending court cases with participants attending my workshops, many times someone will say, "That is just not fair." What they mean is it is not fair that people can be sued because of what they say or do in the workplace. We all have a right to our own opinions. The converse is that we all have a right to earn a living without fear of harassment or discrimination.

To enhance organizational productivity and profitability

More and more organizations are recognizing that the real reason to embark upon any diversity initiative is to contribute to the success of the organization by engaging employees at all levels. By creating an environment that values diversity of all types and helps individuals feel included, the organization enhances its competitiveness in every way. Companies who embark upon diversity for this reason realize quickly that more than training will be necessary.

Sometimes difficult decisions must be made that challenge values and beliefs that were never discussed before in the workplace. For example, Disney and AT&T realized that to help all employees feel included and respected, they needed to recognize same sex couples in their benefits plan. Making the decision to recognize the LGBT community (lesbian, gay, bisexual, transgender) in that way prompted boycotts and negative publicity. Companies today must weigh the loss of business versus gain of potential business and the overall advantages and disadvantages of addressing diversity issues that make some people uncomfortable.

Diversity, therefore, should be addressed just as any other business issue would. By relating to the overall mission and vision of the organization, then analyzing business objectives, diversity initiatives will become much clearer. By evaluating all business issues, several companies have realized that creating a diverse workforce and supporting that workforce manifests employee engagement and leads to the following benefits:

- Lower turnover and higher loyalty

- Reduced employee conflict and tension
- Improved morale
- More effective and innovative teams
- More objective, performance-based criteria used for performance evaluation
- Reduced training costs due to higher retention
- Better client relations
- Improved interdepartmental relations
- Better and more inclusive mentoring and coaching

The bottom line effects of diversity and inclusion has been illustrated, measured, and proven through anecdotal and qualitative research (See the research articles by E. Holly Buttner, Kevin B. Low, and Lenora Billings-Harris). Although diversity entails more than training, that is a good place to start to raise awareness. To make an effective difference, organizations should evaluate the organizational benefits of effectively leveraging diversity, inclusion and engagement and clarify expected results to all concerned. I suggest that you follow the following six major stages.

Six Stages of Diversity Success™

1. Assess need
- identify business objectives
- benchmark best practices
- determine business case for a diversity initiative

2. Analyze
- conduct a baseline survey of employee perceptions regarding diversity, inclusion, and engagement
- correlate results with business operational objectives
- develop visual descriptors (company or department-wide)

3. Develop a diversity strategy and interventions
- educate the organization to create a base of understanding of the business need to leverage diversity and embrace change (company-wide)

4. Evaluate and enhance business systems and processes
- concurrent with awareness & development, evalute H.R. pro-

cesses as well as marketing; community relations; product/service development; and so forth. (task forces)

5. Reassess employee perceptions
* after implementation of various interventions
* resurvey employees and compare results to baseline
* identify success and areas needing further focus
* determine next steps
* (comapny-wide)

6. Evaulate business results
* compare business results to visual descriptors
* determine actions needed to make new behaviors part of the company culture

Stage 1: Assess the Need. Review the organization's business objectives, mission, and goals and determine which of them may be impacted by diversity in a positive or negative way. Conduct an organizational diversity assessment to determine possible issues and concerns surrounding diversity. Do not assume that the people responding to the survey understand what diversity is. Use other words to identify the issues you're targeting. Evaluate the organizational systems such as recruiting, compensation, performance management, and career development. Develop questions about leadership and the overall work environment. As part of the assessment, a diversity council or committee should develop *visual descriptors* to identify what the organization will be once it has achieved its goal of inclusiveness.

A *visual descriptor* is a sentence that describes what people would be saying and doing, and the general attitudes they would have, about the organization after the objective has been achieved.

One client developed visual descriptors for several areas of the business. The following are a few examples:
* Competitors will look to us for best practices in the industr
* Competitors know the best talent wants to work for our organization.
* The leadership demographics reflect worker demographics.
* Employees will feel free to take risks to solve problems.

- Employees are proud to work for our company.
- Work teams are innovative.
- Our employee engagement scores are high.
- Employees know that our leadership listens and supports them
- The community rewards our efforts as a good corporate citizen.
- We are financially successful.
- We have a strong market share, including within emerging markets.
- We are viewed as leaders, not followers, within our industry.

Notice that this list does not focus on ethnicity and gender. When all workers feel valued, respected, and included the resulting behavior of the organization demonstrates strong management practices in general.

Stage 2: Analysis. Analyze the results of the assessment as they compare to business directives and objectives such as increasing market share, turnover, customer satisfaction, and so on. Once this has been completed, then it will become more evident which diversity directives are most urgent.

Stage 3: Awareness. Develop and deliver customized diversity awareness training to all involved, starting at the top. It is imperative that everyone understands why the company is focusing on diversity and inclusion, what it means to the company, and how it affects each employee. The training produces an organizational baseline of understanding of the issues.

Stage 4: Evaluate Business Systems. The most effective approach for evaluating organizational systems is to use one or several teams, often called diversity councils or diversity committees. These teams should have a very specific mission. For example, one team could study and address the perception of leadership; another, development and performance evaluation; another, customer service; another, hiring and retention; another, community relations; and another, targeted marketing. Each team would evaluate the organization's processes and procedures within a specific area and determine whether or not there are barriers or bridges to leveraging diversity.

Stage 5: Evaluation and Re-assessment. To determine if any progress is being made after diversity initiatives have been implemented, an evaluation is necessary. It can take the form of surveys, interviews, or focus groups. After analyzing the results of the evaluation, the next steps can be determined based on the results and your original assessment of business objectives.

Stage 6: Business Results. As a separate evaluation, business results should be analyzed. It is critical to realize, however, that diversity initiatives take a long time to produce a measurable result. Therefore, visual descriptors should be evaluated.

Making a Difference

Within your department or work unit evaluate the following, and note your findings for future reference:

Hiring—Are many different types of people seriously considered for available positions, or are opportunities given only to people who look, act, and speak like the present staff?

Retention—When people with differences are hired (i.e., ethnicity, age, gender, communication style, educational level, etc.) is their length of tenure similar to that of others, or do they leave the organization sooner?

Marketing—Do the organization's marketing materials, annual report, and newsletters reflect the diversity of the workforce via photos, rewards, and feature articles?

Feedback—Are employees asked what they think about issues, and if so does leadership listen and take action when appropriate?

Linking Corporate Diversity Efforts to Community Engagement for Measurable Results
http://goo.gl/NMFbyW

Chapter 10

In Today's Environment of Political Correctness, It's Too Difficult *to* Know What *to* Do.

Isn't it Easier Just to Treat Everybody the Same?

A great coach doesn't try to change a great player. Instead, the coach discovers what is unique, what is great about each player—and then honors it, is happy for it, uses it.

— John Bunn

Yes, it may appear to be easier to treat everyone the same. The reality is that none of us treats everybody exactly the same way. What we really need to do is stop pretending that we treat everyone the same. If you have sisters and brothers, or sons and daughters, ask yourself, do you treat each of them exactly the same way? Do you treat each of your parents exactly the same way? Surely the answer is no. You interact with each individual based on that individual's personality, skills, interests, and so on. That behavior recognizes differences. We need to reveal and expand that understanding and that willingness to adapt to the workplace. In interacting with people this way, we are showing our unconditional acceptance. Although it takes effort, we can be accepting of others more frequently in the workplace if we consciously focus on doing so.

For years leaders were taught to treat everybody the same. The intention in that message was to treat everyone fairly and or with respect. Treating people fairly does not mean treating them the same. The most effective leaders create and enforce fair guidelines in the workplace. Yet they recognize the unique strengths and talents of individuals so that they can create an environment that motivates each individual to work toward his highest level of potential. Think of Phil Jackson, the former coach of the Chicago Bulls and Los Angeles Lakers. Do you suppose he coached Dennis Rodman exactly the same way that he coached Michael Jordan or Scottie Pippin or even Kobe Bryant? I doubt it. The best coaches identify the talent, determine the most motivating environment for that individual, create the environment, and get out of the way. In other words, they train and then empower the individual to do the best she can do.

This is definitely more difficult than treating everyone the same. Many leaders will say to me, "Well, I just use the Golden Rule. Treat other people the way I want to be treated and then I should be safe, right?" Wrong. All of us, regardless of our religious or spiritual upbringing, have learned some variation of the Golden Rule, treat other people the way you wish to be treated. When considering ethics and values, the Golden Rule does work. If I want you to be honest with me, I must be honest with you.

However, when considering interpersonal relationships and general communication, the Golden Rule is completely ineffective because it assumes that the other person wants to be treated the same way I want to be treated. That assumption is wrong most of the time except as it relates to respect and dignity.

From an ethics and values point of view, all of us want respect, all of us want to be treated with dignity regardless of our station in life, and all of us want opportunities that are fair. All of us want to earn enough money to meet and, perhaps, exceed our needs.

Each of us, however, goes about fulfilling those wants and needs differently. The most effective leaders pay close attention and provide the environment that best allows individuals to reach their objectives. Companies today are recognizing more and more that they must treat people differently, yet fairly, in order to provide the type of motivating environment that causes employees to stay constantly engaged. Issues such as childcare, elder care, adoption, male and female parental leave, flex time, job sharing, telecommuting, formalized mentoring, retirement training, and career development training are all being tackled by progressive organizations today. They realize that the more they can accommodate the needs of their workers, the more likely they will keep good people and great talent.

What this really means is that leaders today must consider not only the external, easily determined differences among their workers such as ethnicity, gender, age and job title, but they must also consider the differences in values and perspectives.

Then they must determine a way to honor those differences while coordinating them with the vision, mission, goals, and objectives of the organization. Not an easy task but certainly one that is achievable if the leadership is open to ideas and willing to listen.

Making a Difference

Find out what the interests of your workforce are. There are many ways to gather this information.

1. Conduct focus groups. Allow the senior executives to sit and listen and not give excuses for things not done in the past.
2. Create a formal or "informal" mentoring program that includes people at all levels and includes mentoring non-management/technical positions as well as the more typical management positions.
3. Learn what other companies are doing in your community or other competitors are doing to make their work environment more attractive to employees.
4. Create innovation teams. They go by many names today: performance teams, drive teams, cross-functional teams, and so on. Assign each with a task to identify creative ways to improve productivity by valuing diversity enough to achieve diversity of thought that leads to solutions and innovation.

Articles and Webinars
http://goo.gl/U3fTPO
http://goo.gl/7ZwdeL

CHAPTER 11

WHY CAN'T *the* GENERATIONS GET ALONG?

*The essence of our effort to see that every child
has a chance must be to assure each an equal
opportunity, not to become equal, but to become
different -- to realize whatever unique potential of body, mind and spirit he or she possesses.*
— John Fischer

A LESSER UNDERSTOOD slice of diversity is generational. There are four generations that work side by side in today's organizations. Each generation is its own culture-each with different memories, priorities, motivators and work style. What complicates generational diversity is what complicates all diversity; all of the other layers that make up a human being coexisting with all of the layers that make up a different human being.

Generational diversity is further complicated because it is ambiguous. While a generation is defined as a group of people delineated by certain eras—their generational culture is influenced by social events that occurred during those eras. These groups are thought to have shared memories, and experiences, and perhaps social norms. (However, the age ranges can overlap and we also know that these formative events are almost always considered from an American model of perception.

Furthermore, they do not necessarily take into account the influence of a person's other group identities.)

Researchers have identified four generations currently at work:
Matures, born 1920–1945
Boomers, born 1946–1964
Generation, born X 1965–1980
Millennials, born 1980–2000
(Eras vary depending on source)

Matures

Born before World War II, Matures grew up during or had parents of the Great Depression. The era in which they were contemporized pointed to family bonds and spirituality as rocks in the instability of war and economic depression. Education and vacation were the fruits of hard work and were commonly for the wealthy. For most, home was very important as the source of pleasure and comfort.

The Mature's values include:
Dedication
Sacrifice
Hard Work
Conformity
Law and order
Respect for authority
Patience
Delayed reward
Duty before pleasure
Adherence to rules

Boomers (Baby Boomers)

This generation began during the all-American bliss of the 50s and closed in the storm of the 60's and 70s. While Boomers learned hard work from their parents, disappointed by politicians and the disparate allocation of the American dream, Boomers learned to believe only in themselves. Women began to work and divorce carried on with regularity. Education became more available, instead of for the privileged. And protesting authority was the norm.

The Boomer's values include:
Optimism
Team orientation
Personal gratification
Health and wellness
Personal growth
Youth
Work
Involvement

Generation X

When Generation Xers began working in the 1990s, some doubted their values and work ethics. This was because Gen-Xers grew up more cynical than their forebears. They were the first to see corporate down-sizing and thus were not loyal to the company as were their parents and grandparents. They were the first to describe something called work/life balance. Gen- Xers are thought to ignore authority and to be self-sufficient –an attribute borne out of these, the Latch-key kids of largely divorced parents.

The Gen Xers values include:
  Diversity
  Thinking Globally
  Balance
  Techno-literacy
  Fun
  Informality
  Self-reliance
  Pragmatism

Millennials (Generation Y)

Millennials are those that were born after 1980. This generation was raised on the Internet and is technologically adept. They are multi-task-ers: texting and surfing the Net, and emailing. Using a phone to talk often does not cross their mind as a communication option. They were the first children to have "play dates" and soccer moms—Female Gen-Xers and younger Boomers who off-ramped the corporate latter to have families. This generation is global, connected, and flexible. They are comfortable with diversity and are environmental advocates having grown up with the first electric cars.

The Gen Yers values include:
  Optimism
  Civic duty
  Confidence
  Achievement
  Sociability
  Morality
  Sustainability
  Diversity

Generational differences occur over process, priorities, and of course perspective. Like all diversity, people clash at work when the generational cultures of these groups drive individuals to respond to or prioritize differently—even on non-controversial issues. For example, the Boomers in the company are concerned about their 401Ks and elder care benefits as they care for their aging Mature parents. The Gen-Xers and Millennials have a different set of priorities perhaps, focusing instead on childcare benefits.

A Mature in the office understands the complex social and political network to get an idea in front of an executive because she is long tenured with the company. Her counterpart, a young Millennial wants to by-pass the long-winded process of relationship building and knocks on the CEOs door.

Making a Difference

Explain, Don't Evaluate--Teach employees how to explain their wants and positions in a way that leaves room for another person's truth.

Coach and Train across generations--While a process may be faster (a Millennial Value), relationship building may be wiser and more fruitful over time (Boomer Value). When mediating between generations, explain the virtue and shortcomings of the various approaches. Then work to craft a solution that blends the best of each person's position.

Show appreciation—the speed of the Gen-Xers is good, but it's the third generation of a process that the Mature in the office originally put together. Think of it this way. The iPhone 4 was not an original idea. It was built upon the original iPhone, which was built upon the original cell phone. Look for ways to appreciate everyone's contribution even if that contribution is memory and background someone can bring.

Facilitate discussions focused on the following:
How would a Mature view phrases like:
Environmentally friendly
Play date
OMG; LOL; ROFL; BTW
How would a Boomer view phrases like:
Tele-commuting
God, Country, Family
The husband brings home the bacon; the wife fries it in a pan
How would a Generation Xer view phrases like:
Live to work
Company man
Teamwork
How would a Millenial view phrases like:
Live where the job is
Work to live
Yearly performance appraisals

Webinar : Secrets to Building Generational Harmony http://goo.gl/MhYPZA

Isn't This *a* Free Country? Why Am I Not Free *to* Say What I Really Think *at* Work?

You can only protect your liberties in this world by protecting the other man's freedom. You can only be free if I am free.
— Clarence Darrow

IT IS A PARADOX THAT we live in a country that protects free speech so fiercely, yet some speech is considered inappropriate. The reality is that words do hurt. They do impact productivity in the workplace if repeated often enough.

In the past, many who were affected by hurtful, racist, sexist, or homophobic comments just said nothing. Often they left the company, only to discover that the unacceptable environment existed elsewhere. Today workers are not so willing to keep "grinning and bearing" inappropriate behavior in the workplace. Courts have upheld accusations of "a hostile environment." Often the offending person as well as the company must pay damages to the victim.

Ultimately, everyone wants to have the opportunity to contribute to their fullest degree possible in an environment that respects them.

Showing respect includes taking responsibility for one's own actions and speaking up when inappropriate comments are made. The following poem demonstrates this point.

Who Am I?

Who am I?
I am the Latino teenager who works
part-time in your mailroom.
You know
The one you think is in a gang,
Just because I use street slang.

Who am I?
I'm the Black woman who works
in your group.
You know
The one who wears her hair in braids,
or a natural, or dreadlocks,
the one you call a radical with
an attitude.

Who am I?
I am your blind neighbor.
You know
The one you always speak loudly to
as though I had a hearing disability
instead of one of sightlessness.

Who am I?
I'm the Korean grocer in your
neighborhood.
You know
The one you call unfriendly just
because I don't smile enough for you.

Who am I?
I am a lesbian, or the gay person
who is your associate.
You know . . . oops, maybe you don't know.
I chose not to share that aspect of who I am,
Because you and your friends are
always joking about "Homo's", and
"queers", and "lesbos".
If you only knew how closely I work with you.

Who am I?
I am the Japanese American who
works in your sales department.
You know
The one whose name you make fun of
and expect me to laugh.

Who am I?
I am the Christian woman who travels
with you to make client calls.
You know
The one you keep apologizing to,
every time you tell an off-color joke,
or use God's name in vain.
Why do you apologize?
You obviously are not sorry, or you would
change your behavior.

Who am I?
I am the older man.
You know
The one you get impatient with
because I don't talk, move, or drive
as fast as you do.
One day you to will be old
unless
you experience the only other alternative.

Who am I?
I am your administrative assistant.
You know
The one you always call "Hon" or "Sweetie"
whenever you want coffee.
How many years will it take for you
to learn my real name?

Who am I?
I am the new associate who just
relocated to your office.
You know
The one you imitate all the time
because of my southern accent.

Who am I?
I am the American Indian.
You know

The one you call chief, and ask how's my squaw.
If you were interested in me as an individual,
you would know
that squaw is a derogatory French Canadian term,
and chief is not a word I joke about.

Who am I?
I am the Puerto Rican.
You know
The one who speaks Spanish to my
friends at work.
You think we are talking about you . . .
Don't flatter yourself.

Who am I?
I'm the African American man who
works down the hall.
You know
the one you and your friends say,
I only got my job because of
my color, of course not because I was the
best candidate.

Who am I?
I am the Chinese American human
resource specialist.
You know
The one you keep asking to help you with your computer,
even though I don't understand that technical stuff either.

Who am I?
I am a White American.
You know
The one you blame for the errors
made over 200 years ago
the one you think "has it made"
the one you think "just doesn't get it"
even though I am your strongest
advocate among my peers.

Who am I?
I am an American person
I worry about the environment,
education for my children, my next
paycheck, crime, and crabgrass
in my front yard.
I am the person who wants to know
the real you, if only you would act
interested in the real me.

—Lenora Billings-Harris

Making A Difference

Listen … really concentrate on the messages you hear throughout the day. Record below:
—The stereotypical judgments you make of others
—The stereotypes you hear from others
Make a commitment to yourself. For the next seven days, do not accept stereotypes as truth. Tell your inner/ego voice, "Thanks but no thanks," when it makes a stereotypical or biased statement, then search for the facts. When someone else utters stereotypical comments, ask, in a polite way, "Why do you think that is so?" Sometimes just a question can raise awareness.

Who Am I?
http://goo.gl/INi0EX

CHAPTER 13

WHAT ARE *the* OFFENSIVE STATEMENTS PEOPLE SAY, ACCIDENTALLY?

Tact is the ability to describe others as they see themselves.
— Eleanor Chaffee

HAVE YOU EVER WISHED you could change the behavior of others when they are referring to a group to which you belong? Often people say and do things without intending to be offensive, but the outcome is discomforting nevertheless. As a result of a group exercise I frequently use in diversity awareness workshops, many participants are enlightened by their associates regarding the pain caused by words and actions not usually intended to hurt. The lists below were developed by many small groups of people, who are members of the group being discussed.

You may see contradictions within lists. Remember, everyone is unique, and has the right to their own opinion. I share this to help you identify the words, actions, and stereotypes that you may wish to discontinue using. By avoiding these terms and selecting more inclusive ways to show respect, you are on the road to building bridges to understanding and an environment conducive to more effective teamwork and one-on-one relations with others.

Religion
I never want to hear...
> I can't have fun, because I am religious.
> I can't think for myself, I must check with the church, Pope, etc.
> I should stop referring to God when at work.
> I am constantly trying to recruit or convert others.
> all born-again Christians are self-righteous and narrow-minded.

I never want to see...
> another church being burned due to hatred.
> another war fought under the shield of religion.

I never want to experience...
> discrimination due to religious or spiritual beliefs.
> one religion judging another as "not as good as."

Sexual Orientation

I never want to see...
> someone "out" a gay person. It is up to the individual to decide with whom to discuss sexuality.
> a straight man imitate a gay man by making hand and wrist gestures.

I never want to hear...
> "Don't ask, don't tell." – (Note: This military regulation was abolished in 2011)
> "Don't be so political!"
> that homosexuality is a choice—it is not. Do heterosexuals choose to be straight?
> it just takes the "right" heterosexual to make a gay or lesbian straight.
> "You just haven't found the right man or woman yet."
> gay men are feminine and lesbian women are "butch."
> "What a waste!" when referring to LGBTs.
> a person's sexual orientation used as part of the description of the person, like, "The gay guy..."
> heterosexual persons say that LGBT persons are sexually interested in them just because they are of the same gender. (We can appreciate the attractiveness of a person without it being sexual, just as heterosexuals can recognize attractive homosexual or heterosexuals, without being sexually attracted to them.)
> someone trying to find out why someone "turned" gay. (We just are.)
> the words "faggot", "fag", "bull-dike", "butch", or "fern".
> others say, "Just don't flaunt it." (Straights flaunt their sexuality all the time.)

I never want to experience...

being asked who the "husband" in the relationship is.

someone saying to me, "Gee, you don't look gay."

being afraid to walk down the street, or participate in gay pride events, for fear of being attacked.

African American
I never want to see...

people grab their purse tighter, just because a Black man is walking in their direction.

police brutality or harassment toward people just because of the color of their skin.

bi-racial couples being stared at or verbally abused.

African American children being abused by teachers, for example, writing on their face with permanent markers.

I never want to hear...

"There goes the neighborhood."

"You don't sound Black!"

"We are in the 'wrong' neighborhood,'" when driving a nice car or just walking down the street.

that a multi-ethnic child was told her existence was a mistake.

comments that African Americans are lazy and on welfare.

African American men are irresponsible.

"Go back to Africa, where you came from." I was born in the United States.

comments that all African Americans come from the ghetto.

African Americans are not patriotic.

all African American young men are gang bangers.

"I know how she or he got her or his job!"

Hispanic/Mexican/Latino
I never want to see...

the Mexican tourist trinket of a man sleeping at the foot of a tree.

We are hard workers. This symbolizes laziness.

the term *Hispanic*. I am Dominican and proud of it.

Hispanic laborers being mistreated.

I never want to hear...

the term wetbacks.

"Are you legal?"

"Don't speak Spanish at work." We are often discussing work.

Illegal aliens – Undocumented workers is better.

I never want to experience...

being harassed by police.

feeling ashamed because I speak Spanish.

American Indian (Native American)

I never want to hear...

the word squaw. It is not an Indian word, and it is very derogatory.

we are too sensitive. Get over it.

that all Native Americans are drunks and live on reservations.

"You can't do that! This is a hospital!" (when practicing healing rituals).

"Do you own a casino?"

I never want to see...

our ancestral artifacts stolen or treated with disrespect.

derogatory caricatures of American Indians as sports team mascots.

non-Indians acting as though they are in movies.

Asian

I never want to hear...

"Asian." Take the time to ask to which nationality you are referring.

all Asians are terrible drivers.

all Asians are smart.

"Jap."

"Go back to your country." Many of our ancestors helped build the United States.

I never want to see...

others making fun of the shape of our eyes.

European American/White
I never want to hear...
> your problems are my fault.
> "You just don't get it."
> "All Whites are bigots."

I never want to see...
> discrimination towards anyone, regardless of race.
> people burning the flag.

I never want to experience...
>   loss of our freedoms.

People with Disabilities
I never want to hear...
> "You can't..."
> "Handicapped."

I never want to see...
> people with disabilities being stared at.
> people making fun of us.

I never want to experience...
> job discrimination.
> not being able to get on a bus due to lack of proper equipment on
>   the bus.
> being talked at as though I am not present.

Women
I never want to hear...
> "When are you going to have a baby?"
> "When are you going to get married?"
> women are the weaker sex.
> we are poor money managers.
> "I know why you got that job!"

I never want to see...
> women or girls being verbally or physically abused.
> women "killing" themselves to be thin.
> women being passed over for certain jobs because they are not
>   pretty enough.

I never want to experience...
> discrimination.
> domestic abuse.
> less than equal pay for equal work.

Men
I never want to hear...
> all men are pigs.
> men are insensitive.
> "You've got it so easy."

I never want to see...
> men harassing anyone.
> men being passed over because of Affirmative Action.

Making a Difference

Form a small group of colleagues to explore the pain of stereotypical thinking. Have each member share the following information:

Describe a time in your childhood when you didn't fit in. What was the situation; how did you feel; how did you react?

Discuss the comments listed on the previous pages. For the groups of which you are a member, share what you never want to see, hear or experience.

Articles and Webinars
http://goo.gl/U3fTPO
http://goo.gl/7ZwdeL

WHAT ARE *the* HABITS *of* LEADERS WHO CREATE *and* SUSTAIN *an* ENVIRONMENT *that* SUPPORTS DIVERSITY?

Diversity: The art of thinking independently together.

— Malcom Forbes

THINK OF A LEADER/MANAGER in your life who really motivated you to be the best you could be. What attributes or characteristics describe her? What habits did he have that worked for you? I have asked hundreds of leaders this question. Here is a sampling of the most frequent answers.

He or she:
> Was fair and respectful toward others.
> Had high personal standards.
> Believed in my abilities and potential.
> Helped me believe in myself.
> Encouraged and stretched me.
> Led by example.
> Mentored and coached.
> Asked for and appreciated different points of view.
> Listened.
> Criticized objectively.
> Had integrity; was honorable.
> Helped me solve my own problems.
> Had a vision.
> Developed a trusting environment.

The specific word, diversity, was rarely used when people described their best, favorite, or most effective manager, unless the subordinate person was in an underrepresented group. However, fairness, respect, objectiveness, and listening recurred frequently.

These attributes describe an effective manager and leader. The key within a diverse environment is to be able to practice these behaviors with all workers, rather than only employees with whom you are most comfortable. Developing the diversity leadership dimension requires a commitment to demonstrate the following cultural competencies on a regular basis:

Learn each individual's professional aspirations and support their efforts to reach them. Many organizations have some type of career development or succession planning process. In order to make these programs more effective within a diverse environment, be sure that you are talking to all of your staff about their career aspirations. Even if your organization does not have many opportunities for individuals looking for upward mobility, your interest in their career and your assistance in their development will be greatly appreciated and usually motivates people to do their best work. If there are no opportunities within the organization and the employee ultimately leaves the company, the company then has a positive ambassador in the overall community.

Create opportunities for highly talented employees to be exposed to leaders who may not otherwise interact with them. Create opportunities where they present a report, attend a meeting in your place, or do various other things whereby they can interact with leaders in the organization who, if impressed, can impact their career in a positive way.

Create cross-functional teams. As organizations have downsized, right-sized, and re-engineered their businesses, many management positions have been eliminated, thus requiring groups to work together as teams in order to complete the necessary tasks. When you create cross-functional teams, ideas flourish. People are exposed to each other and discover that different departments have different viewpoints, and that is beneficial to the overall innovation potential of the organization. When creating these teams, remember that putting people together does not automatically make them a team. Attention does need to be given to developing that group of people into an effective, productive, trusting team.

Volunteer for community projects that teach understanding and acceptance, both directly and indirectly. By doing this, you set the example that you are continually enhancing your understanding and appreciation of people different than you. That behavior can encourage others within the organization to do the same. For example, you may choose to become a mentor within the Big Brothers/Big Sisters organization. This can enable you to better understand young people. The experience can teach humility, and patience, and it can certainly will help you appreciate what is important to people whose backgrounds may be different than yours. These learnings have great application once you are at work, interacting with your staff day to day.

Delegate fairly. Sometimes we have a tendency to delegate to the same people all the time because they do good work and we know things will be done well. However, if we are going to truly develop each staff member, regardless of their packaging, we need to identify projects, tasks, and responsibilities that could further develop their skills. Once the task is delegated, be sure to coach and counsel, and be clear regarding your expectations regarding process and outcomes.

Communicate and support intolerance of inappropriate and disrespectful behavior. This must be an ongoing activity, one where you are constantly looking for opportunities to reflect respect of others within the workplace.

Evaluate performance objectively. Employees really want to do a good job. The problem is that often they don't know what a good job is because the clues from management and leadership are unclear. As soon as a person joins an organization, she or he should be given a clear job description, and the specific goals and objectives for that individual should be developed. The criteria for measurement should be clarified. Throughout the evaluation period, feedback should be given so that when the evaluation review is actually conducted, neither the manager nor the employee is surprised by the results. When considering generational diversity, one of the biggest complaints from Millennials (Gen Y) is that they are not given enough feedback regarding how they are doing. Once a year is not enough.

It is not easy being totally objective all the time. However, if the skills and expectations for the job are clear, the measurement criteria is clear, and the feedback is continuous, then it becomes easier for you to be fair with each employee.

Consider individual needs when enforcing company policies and guidelines. The idea is to be fair. However, "fair" does not necessarily mean "the same." There are times when you have to decide how to implement policies without showing favoritism while recognizing differences. An example might be with work schedules. Although within a department, and within the same job category, everyone is probably expected to arrive

at the same time and leave at the same time, it would be appropriate, when necessary, to allow flex-time as long as it is clear that the total amount of time required for work is covered. Job sharing is also helpful here. If parents have child-related issues, effective managers consider those issues and determine whether or not exceptions are necessary while balancing the effect of making those exceptions and their impact on the overall department. Tele- commuting is not only becoming more common place. Research indicates that people are more productive, when they work from home.

Rather than try to come up with the best idea alone, solicit input from the employees involved and from other managers to determine what the most appropriate action is. This practice engages everyone and often makes the solution more accepted by the full work team.

You may have noticed that nowhere in this chapter have I mentioned doing things based on ethnicity, gender, disability, age, and the like.

It is critical that effective leaders and managers realize that everyone in the organization contributes to its diversity. The more you are able to connect with individuals, the more you will be able to create an environment that causes them to produce at their highest level, regardless of their packaging.

Making a Difference

1. **Make time to talk privately with each of your employees on a regular basis**. For example, if you have 10 employees, provide each with 30 minutes every two weeks where

they have the opportunity to share with you whatever they wish. They can ask any questions, give you ideas, and you have the opportunity to get to know them personally and coach and counsel them as necessary.

2. **Ask your staff, individually, how they would prefer to be managed and how they would prefer to be rewarded.** Often we assume money is what everyone wants. This is not necessarily true. Money is almost never theprimary reason people quit a job. Using learning assessments such as the DiSC Profile or other tools to better understand communication styles and the ingredients for the most motivating environments for different styles can be very helpful for both you and the employee. When you ask an employee how he or she wishes to be rewarded, you may discover personal interests, and professional aspirations that you can be supportive of. For example, perhaps one employee might be most motivated by having the com - pany pay part of her child's tuition. A child-free person may be most appreciative if the company provided additional vacation time so that he could visit a favorite place.

3. **Take your staff to lunch every now and then, just to chat.** The more actions you take to demonstrate sincere interest in the individual, the more likely your staff will want to "go the extra mile." The challenge is to be able to make the time. However, once you do, you will be more likely to see the real person, instead of just their "packaging." Their differences will then be an asset instead of a barrier.

Article
Diversity Collisions in the Workplace: Silo Mentality versus the Networked Reality
http://goo.gl/w5P3b7

As *a* Leader, I'm Held Accountable *for* Cost. I Can't Afford *to* Hire *the* Disabled, Can I?

Alone we can do so little; together we can do so much.

— Helen Keller

ONE OF THE MYTHS THAT surround people with disabilities is that the employing organization has to take extraordinary and costly measures to accommodate their needs in the workplace. This is truly a myth. Many people with disabilities require no special adjustments and others require very few. The problem is that hiring managers allow their fears, discomforts, and biases to get in the way of making objective decisions about the skills, talents, and abilities of a person with a major disability.

Not hiring people with disabilities is costly. A few years ago, The President's Committee on Employment of People with Disabilities conducted a study that indicated that, at that time, there were 20 million people with disabilities who were of working age (16 to 65). Of those 20 million, 14 million wanted to work. Of that 14 million, 9 million were unemployed. Although the Americans with Disabilities Act makes it illegal to discriminate against a person with disabilities, the practice still goes on. Biases and stereotypes get in the way just as it does with other people with visible differences.

Over the past 20+ years, I have made presentations to and conducted training for thousands of people. To this day, I still can count only a very few participants who were in my audience, employed by my clients, who happened to have disabilities. Corporations and society in general, are not intentionally biased. However, we fear that which we don't know, and we rely on myths when we have no factual information. Without the facts, people assume that a person with disabilities simply cannot do certain jobs. Yet all of us have seen individuals on television, and some of us have experienced firsthand, people who have disabilities performing the same types of jobs that able-bodied people do.

As a professional speaker, and diversity strategist, I am required to travel extensively, to speak to groups, to use AV equipment, and so on. Within my profession alone, there are many people who happen to have disabilities who do the same things I do. There are several keynote speakers who are blind, who use a wheelchair, and who have hearing impairments or other disabilities. The limitations are only in the mind of the uninformed.

The question of cost is an interesting one because, in fact, it costs more money not to employ people with disabilities. Certainly those 9 million who are not employed even though they want to work, still have to eat and sleep. Without employment, many must rely on public assistance. The government supports public assistance. The government is paid for by "we, the people." Wouldn't it make more sense to provide more opportunities for individuals who happen to have a disability to be gainfully employed?

Going beyond one's biases is not easy in this case. It requires accepting that we have biases. I worked for a car dealership for a short period of time, and to the amazement of many, one of the sales consultants was a person who used a wheelchair. Most sales managers would argue, when I would share this story during presentations, that this individual could not perform a very important step in the sales process, which is conducting the demonstration drive. Because of that assumption, many times he was turned down for automotive sales positions.

One of the problems is that the hiring managers rarely ask candidates how they would perform a required step in the job that appears to be one that they would not be able to do. Managers assume that "reasonable accommodations" require thousands and thousands of dollars.

In this case, the dealership did not have to spend any money at all. Since this particular sales department was set up as teams, the team worked out the details of how best to satisfy the requirement of taking all customers on a demo drive, even though it would be impractical to fit each car for handicapped accessibility. In other words, when Pat reached that step in the sales process, he would T.O., as it's said in the business (turnover), his customer to one of his team members who would accompany the customer. When the customer and the team member returned to the dealership, Pat would resume the negotiation process. Internal to the dealership, this is a critical step in the sales process. This is the time when the sales consultant begins to really determine if the customer loves this car, is ready to buy, or perhaps, should be shown other alternatives. Obviously, Pat would not be able to see those signals, but his team member could. Had Pat chosen to sue the dealerships that turned him down, the courts would probably see this step simply as an internal detail that could be worked out, rather than a clear job requirement that could not be performed by a person in a wheelchair. Not only was Pat able to perform his job, he was often Salesperson of the Month.

While conducting a diversity workshop, I was thrilled to have as a participant an individual who was completely deaf. Many times during keynote presentations, I have people with hearing disabilities in the audience, but I had never had the experience of such a participant in a training session, which had many small group discussions, team activities, and the like. Two interpreters accompanied this participant for the entire seven-hour program and Signed everything. It was fascinating to watch the other participants' reaction to having the individual in class. I thought, "My, this organization is progressive," because they had employed this individual for 15 years. Unfortunately, however, his perspective was different.

"They never ask me about my career aspirations. They assume I can only do the specific job they originally hired me for. They complain when I do the same things other employees do, like attend training, because it costs them money. [In this organization, all employees are required to receive 40 hours of training per year.] When I attend training classes, they must employ two interpreters, which cost $50 per hour, each. They never seem to realize that my participation in these seminars improves my skills and abilities, enables me to interact with others, just like any other employee. If they didn't complain so much, it would boost my motivation and perhaps I'd be even more productive when I go back to work."

Another client is a customer service center. The employees answer a 1-800 line to process the repair claims for customers of a particular appliance. Since the responsibilities require workers to sit at a computer terminal, being ambulatory by foot is not required. The organization regularly works with habilitation centers around the city to identify individuals with the skills to perform these duties. One would think this would be a great job for some people who use wheelchairs.

The organization's challenge is not finding people who can do the job, but rather it is getting them to the job. In most communities today, public buses have lifts for people who need them.

However, most people who use wheelchairs have told me that the lifts frequently do not work, or there is insufficient funding to equip enough buses to accommodate their needs. One individual told me he had to wait two hours before a bus finally had a lift that worked. Imagine if you could not predict what time you would arrive at work because the transportation you required frequently was non-operational. Some of you would say, "Well, they should purchase a car that can accommodate their needs." That proposition is extremely expensive and if the person is not employed, from where will the money come?

Because people are so uncomfortable around others who are different in this way, people show their discomfort in amusing, and sometimes annoying, ways. Have you ever talked louder when speaking to a blind person as though that would help him see you? Have you ever "helped" a person in a wheelchair without asking her first? Often I am told people will try to help and then become angered when the person with the disability says, "No, thank you." Perhaps we should put ourselves in their position. If a person uses a wheelchair, most likely he or she knows how to manipulate it correctly. So, the reason the person with the disability may say, "No, thank you" could be stemming from safety issues. Perhaps it is, in fact, easier for them to simply do things for themselves rather than watching us trip over ourselves trying to be helpful.

The government has been an excellent example of how to be insensitive when dealing with people with disabilities. The word handicapped is stamped all over the place. Yet, most people know that using that particular word is not favored. Perhaps understanding the reason would be helpful in motivating people to avoid such a word. Handicapped originated from the British term that identified people who could legally beg for money in public, centuries ago. If persons were disabled, they could legally beg for money in public by holding a cap in hand. Thus, the word handicapped implies that people with disabilities are begging. Certainly, they are not. Just like others with differences, they are simply requesting an opportunity to utilize their skills, abilities, and talents and be treated with dignity regardless of their packaging.

Organizations such as the Holiday Inn and McDonalds have been recognized over the past several years for their efforts to employ people with disabilities, both physical and developmental. As the skilled labor pool continues to shrink, yet higher skill levels are needed. Wouldn't it make sense for organizations to more clearly and objectively identify the skills and abilities needed and hire people who can perform those skills regardless of their packaging?

Salt River Project, a utility company in Arizona, works closely with the habilitation center to employ people who are physically or developmentally disabled in their reclamation efforts. The Salt River Project salvages as much wasted material as possible to reduce the cost of utilities and to save the environment. Since working in cooperation with the habilitation center, they have realized two things: the employees are thrilled to have the opportunity to work productively, and the employees of SRP continually raise their level of awareness and understanding of the many skills and talents of all individuals. Creating work opportunities for people with disabilities is not just the right thing to do, it is the economic thing to do.

Making a Difference

There are several actions you can take to raise your level of understanding and acceptance of people with disabilities. Try these suggestions and record your reactions:

Wear a blindfold for an hour or two and have a friend or colleague lead you around the workplace. Afterwards, record your reactions. Were you trusting? Were you fearful? Were there many hazards?

Rent a wheelchair and then go to a shopping mall. Notice how people react to you. Do they look at you when they speak or do they look at a friend who is accompanying you most of the time? How easy or difficult is it to get around? Try using the rest room.

Place a telephone call using a specially equipped phone for people with hearing impairments (TDD).

Become a volunteer for community organizations that provide services to people with disabilities, such as cerebral palsy or multiple sclerosis. Record your reactions and learnings.

Articles and Webinars
http://goo.gl/U3fTPO
http://goo.gl/7ZwdeL

Chapter 16

Overcoming Barriers *on* Our Journey Toward Achieving Cultural Competence

You must become the change you wish to see in the world.

— Gandhi

There are barriers, booby traps, and blocked roadways on our journey toward achieving cultural competence. What do you say to the White co-worker who always wants to touch your locks or braids? How do you tell your manager to stop giving you a high-five every time he agrees with something you say? The biggest barrier to giving feedback in these type situations is the fear most people have when it comes to speaking up in a respectful way to encourage others to stop insensitive or inappropriate behavior. One of the major reasons people do not speak up more often when they experience inappropriate behavior is because they do not know how to speak up when they have to interact with the offender on a regular basis. If the offender is your manager speaking up may seem too dangerous. If the offender is a colleague in your department, well it is easier just to be silent. Or is it? That silence perpetuates inappropriate behavior.

Each of us, if we really choose to make a difference, must be unwilling to be a part of the silent majority on this issue. The following is a four-step process for giving feedback that is easy to understand but takes practice to implement successfully. Once you have mastered it, try teaching it to your children, if you have any, and watch how they will take control of their own challenges more often than not. The process is called **S.T.O.P**™.

S—State the inappropriate behavior objectively and unemotionally. When beginning this feedback, describe the specific behavior you want the offender to stop doing or saying. Your words need to be stated in a nonjudgmental, objective, unemotional way. Too often when we do speak up regarding inappropriate behavior we are emotional, we show our anger, and we start with feelings and blame. This often causes the offender to become defensive or to go into denial mood. In order to maintain your objectivity and to assure the offender clearly understands what you are referring to, simply state what he or she has done. If you cannot measure it, it probably is not clear enough to approach the offender.

By the way, this only works with specific behaviors not opinions or beliefs. You would not be able to convert a Democrat to a Republican or Libertarian using this technique, because you would be judging beliefs and attitudes.

T—Tell the offender how you feel when she or he performs this inappropriate behavior.

It is important that you state your feelings not your opinion. Opinions are judgments in disguise, so the offender may shut down the moment you judge their behavior. Does it make you angry? Hurt? Excluded? Offended? Most people have a tough time identifying exactly what they are feeling. You may need to Google "unpleasant feelings" to get help.

O—Options, options, options.

Provide alternative behavioral suggestions. Frequently, when we tell others to stop doing something, we don't tell them what we would prefer instead.

P—Positive results.

Share with the offender what would be in it for her if she chooses to change behavior. Each of us behaves based on "what's in it for me."

It is important that you answer this question. Change does not occur unless there is a reason. If the individual cannot see a good reason to change behavior, the inappropriate behavior usually continues. If the inappropriate behavior also breaks company policy, the consequences, should the person choose not to change his or her behavior, could be a disciplinary one by the company. However, as often as possible when using this technique, try not to threaten the person at this step. Rather, show positive, interpersonal relationship results should he or she choose to change his or her behavior. Ask her if she is 'willing to work with you on this.' Get her commitment.

Several years ago, after having taught this technique many times, I was faced with a personal situation where I had to walk my talk. A very close friend had the habit of using the term faggot often. Whenever he was referring to someone he did not like or someone who showed effeminate behavior, he would use this label. I find the term very offensive so I realized I needed to use the S.T.O.P. technique. Just like most people, initially I was hesitant. This individual was, and today still is, a very dear friend. I did not want to offend him or create any situation that would interfere with our friendship. He and his girlfriend were among six of us that often socialized together; my husband and I, he and his girlfriend, and another couple. Let's call him Walter.

While the six of us were enjoying a sunny and hot weekend afternoon in Phoenix, Walter used the word. I had informed my husband earlier that if Walter used that term again, I would need to speak with him. I did not want my husband to be surprised nor caught off guard should things not go well. I waited for Walter to be in a situation where he and I could talk privately. Eventually, when he entered the kitchen to help himself to refreshments, I followed him. This technique only takes about 45 seconds. It is not intended that the offender respond at that time. What is important is that you get your points across quickly, non-judgmentally, and clearly. Here's what happened:

"Walter, when you use the word 'faggot' [step one—S] it offends me. I am very uncomfortable in your presence [step two—T]. I would prefer that, if you must use a descriptor of this kind, you use words that are more appropriate, such as gay, lesbian, etc. Actually, I would prefer that you not use a term at all unless you know, for a fact, that the individual happens to be LGBT and that piece of information is pertinent to the story you are sharing with us at the time [step three—O]. If you are willing to change your behavior in this way, at least in my presence, you certainly will be more welcome in our home [step four—P]. This invisible barrier that has come up between us will dissipate, and you, then, can tell your wonderful stories without any concern of offending me or anyone else in the group."

Walter responded by not responding at all. He had a stunned look on his face. He walked away, went back outside, and dove into the pool.

I thought, "Oh well. No change here." However, I was wrong.

Shortly thereafter when he and his girlfriend and the other couple went out to dinner, he shared this experience with them. It was not complimentary to me. Apparently, however, no one took his side even though I had not shared with anyone what I had done. Although they didn't criticize him, they didn't support the labels that he was, at least momentarily, using to describe me. I learned of this interaction from one of the four other individuals.

The next several times that Walter and I were in each other's company, I noticed that he did not use that term. I made it a point to let him know that I noticed his changed behavior and how much I appreciated it. I did this in private. Several months later, when chatting with one of the other members of this party of friends, I was told that Walter no longer used the term in their presence either. A few months later, I was talking to another member of this group about diversity training in general. This member works for an organization that has many diversity initiatives in place and I'm always interested in learning what they are doing. Her husband works with Walter.

She told me, and I later confirmed it with her husband, that indeed, Walter no longer used this term at work.

The point is this; the feedback took approximately 45 seconds.

My objective was to get Walter to stop using that word, at least in my presence. I exceeded my objective and change occurred. I cannot guarantee that every time you use this process you will have similar results. However, you will never know the impact you, as one individual, can have on another individual unless you try.

Making a Difference

The best way to utilize this technique is to initially use it in a non- threatening environment.

Use the S.T.O.P. technique when giving feedback to a child regarding any type of inappropriate behavior. Once you have gotten comfortable with the process, then attempt it with others.

Plan what you will say ahead of time. Writing it out might be helpful so that you can focus your thoughts, stay objective, and identify options. Always close the techniques by saying, "Are you willing to help me with this?"

Be sure you're in a private place when you walk through these steps. If the offender does become defensive or goes into denial, simply repeat the process calmly, or reschedule a time to chat.

Be sure to recognize and show appreciation for changed behavior as quickly as possible so the person knows this was, and is, important to you and that you appreciate their efforts.

Webinar: Get Along Much? 3 Practical Ways to Approach People Problems http://goo.gl/K6brx6

CHAPTER 17

CAN ONE PERSON MAKE *a* DIFFERENCE?

*Injustice anywhere is a threat to justice every-
where.*

— Rev. Dr. Martin Luther King, Jr.

AS WE ANALYZE THE MANY challenges present in our society when
interacting with the many differences among us all, it can sometimes
seem overwhelming. It can seem as though one person cannot make a
difference. I believe that each of us, individually, can make a tremen-
dous difference.

No major social change has ever occurred because the masses, all
of a sudden, decided it was a good thing to do. Consider the works of
Gandhi, Mother Teresa, Martin Luther King Jr., Susan B. Anthony,
Jesus, Nelson Mandela, Irena Sendler, Lech Walesa, and others. Each
of them had a strong belief and commitment. Each of them was able
to make major changes. You, too, in your own way, can change your
community, your workplace, and the overall respect and acceptance of
people on this planet.

In order to continue this journey of valuing diversity, you need three
things. You already possess all three.

Each of us has a sub-conscious behavior guide. It is represented by the
inner voice that is constantly telling us what to do and what to believe.

The first level—**The Protector**—represents our mask or façade. We
use it when we most want to be accepted. It tells us to act this way or
that, depending on what will be accepted by those around us at the time.
We all must wear a façade sometime in order to fit in. Some people are
forced to wear this mask, even when they would rather not, because
those in power make rules for those who are not. The rules are often
based on what makes the powerful comfortable, not what makes the
most sense or what is most respectful of individuals. For example, many
men and women wear suits to work, not because they really want to,
but because their work culture dictates that suits will enable them to be

taken seriously and look like they have potential. There is nothing wrong with wearing suits. However, clothes do not, by themselves, indicate a person's ability to get the job done well. Because wearing something other than a suit would be risky, many people just follow the norm.

The second level is **The Judge**. When we are at this level we are motivated to be right. It's the ego speaking. This is the most dangerous of the three because most people rarely examine the messages here. They therefore act without thought. Values and beliefs reside here, along with biases, stereotypes, and prejudice. Unexamined, these messages affect how we treat others, and what we believe about others. Do you know someone who must be right all the time? They are stuck at the Judge level. We depend on this level most often when we are afraid or stressed. At work, if you are afraid of what your superiors think of you, or are afraid of losing your job to downsizing, rightsizing, or other euphemistic terms for firing people, you might be reacting to messages at this level. We don't think of all the stereotypes at once, only the ones we need. Many of the previous stories in this book demonstrate how we use the information at this level.

Although we need beliefs and values, we need to examine them once in a while to determine whether they still fit. For example, many people were taught as children to "clean their plate, eat all their food." Perhaps if more adults would realize that message no longer is necessary, there would be fewer people needing to go on diets. The value we were supposed to learn was not to waste. We learned it through a behavior that is no longer needed to maintain the value. All of our values and beliefs are connected to behaviors.

When we are so focused on being right, we lose the willingness to understand others and appreciate different ways of thinking and behaving.

The third level is **The Authenticator**. Our motivation is just "to be". Unfortunately, as adults we are not at this level much because we are so busy judging or worrying about being judged. At this level we are willing to accept others regardless of their packaging. We evaluate situations and people based on facts, instead of relying on stereotypes. Children tend to be at this level until they learn the messages that adults pass on to them. This is the level that truly is able to value the diversity of people without judging.

Subconscious Behavior Guide

Let me demonstrate how the model works through an analogy of The Wizard of Oz.

Dorothy was tired of being in Kansas. She wanted to explore.

Dorothy actually represents a change agent. A change agent is someone who is willing to make change happen, often by exploring new and unknown territory. Dorothy was willing to explore. She landed in Munchkin Land.

The Munchkins had never seen a Dorothy before so they relied on their Judge and stereotyped her. They thought she was a good witch. It was to her advantage because she was treated very well, she had privilege. Even though she was treated well, she was being treated as something she was not. No matter how good the treatment, it is always uncomfortable to wear a façade. So, eventually, she wanted to return to Kansas to see Auntie Em.

The Munchkins did not know where Kansas was, but they knew of a wise man named the Wizard. So, they said to Dorothy, "Follow the yellow-brick road. Follow the yellow-brick road." They instructed her to look for the Land of Oz. Living there would be the Wizard.

Dorothy proceeded down the yellow-brick road, and after a short time, she came upon a cornfield. In that cornfield was a scarecrow, unfortunately with crows sitting on his arms. He obviously was not very effective. Dorothy helped the scarecrow down and told him of her journey to the Land of Oz, to find the Wizard. The scarecrow was intrigued and he said, "I could be a much better scarecrow if only I had a brain!" (Because he thought he had no brain, he was flimsy and ineffective.) Dorothy suggested that the scarecrow come with her. You see, Dorothy did not care what the team member looked like as long as he was moving in the same direction as she. As long as he wanted to achieve the same goal, perhaps he could be of help.

They continued down the yellow-brick road a little bit farther and soon came upon the Tin Man. The Tin Man had been neglected by others for years. You see, he looked a little too different. Dorothy and the scarecrow proceeded to tell the Tin Man about the Land of Oz and this man called the Wizard. The Tin Man then said, "I would be a much better Tin Man if only I had a heart." (Perhaps his rigidity was due to his perceived lack of heart.) Dorothy said, "The Wizard, Oz. Come on with us." They proceeded down the yellow-brick road.

They eventually came upon a forest and the trees were rattling. From behind the trees jumped the Cowardly Lion. They told the Cowardly Lion their story, and the lion said, "I would be king of the jungle if only I had courage!" (Because he did not follow his own convictions, he was intimidated by anyone who did, thus always a follower.) Dorothy invited the lion to join their team and find the Wizard in the Land of Oz.

So the four of them, plus Toto, trekked through many perils and eventually arrived at Emerald City. They knocked on the door. As powerful as the Wizard was, he too did not believe he would be accepted just as he was. He too wore a mask, his Protector. He was a very smart man, however. He knew that if he told them they had a brain, a heart, and courage, they would not believe him. They had to experience it.

It is the same as you now having begun to experience the journey of valuing diversity. You could have watched a videotape, or just read one or two chapters of this book.

Diversity and inclusion, however, have to be experienced to be understood so your journey has just begun.

The Wizard informed Dorothy, the scarecrow, the Tin Man, and the lion that they would need to get the broom of the wicked witch, (she represents the obstacles in our lives) and he sent them off on their task. They used their brain, heart, and courage, and came back with the broom. It took Toto, the dog, (The Authenticator) to discover the real Wizard. Toto, represents the innocence and truthfulness of children. Hate has to be carefully taught. Children begin their lives without judgment and ask questions to seek the truth. He represents unconditional acceptance.

The Wizard informed them that they had a brain, a heart, and courage all the time. Here's how these three ingredients relate to you.

You have a brain. Certainly, you had that before you began to read this book. A brain alone, however, is not enough, because a brain alone looks for the most efficient answers to puzzles. The most efficient answers are often stereotypical and biased. They are quick but incorrect. Just using our brain can lead us, ultimately, to tyranny because it will rely on the messages within the Judge. A brain by itself wants to be right, and if I am right, that makes you wrong, which immediately begins a conflict.

So you must connect your brain to your heart. By doing so, you will be empowered to become more patient, to be willing to listen to other points of view, to be less fearful of the unknown, and to be more willing to understand.

A brain and a heart alone are still not quite enough because they do not move you to action. Of the three, courage is the most important. By using your courage, you will be more willing to ask questions, more capable of speaking up against inappropriate behavior and wrongful actions, more determined to have a voice rather than following the silent majority.

CHAPTER 18

How Can I Successfully Perform *with* Global Teams?

I feel we are all islands—in a common sea.

— Anne Morrow Lindbergh

WHILE THE WORKFORCE has indeed shrunk as predictions of 10+ years ago have indicated, the shrinkage has not been entirely for the reasons expected (i.e., outsourcing and various forms of retirement). While these are still significant factors, the economic downturn that has forced many employees out of their positions and their companies earlier than expected has added to this shift. As a result, a saturation of talent that is not likely to subside anytime soon has occurred in many disciplines and industries. Having a global mindset is a key skill. It's not a nice to have; it's a must have.
(excerpt from *TRAILBLAZERS:* How Top Business Leaders are Accelerating Results through Inclusion and Diversity)

LEADERS, MANAGERS AND individual professionals have to be more savy regarding topics pertaining to culture, politics, and country laws when dealing with colleagues around the globe. High levels of cultural competency help avoid mistakes that could cost millions and conversely cross-cultural competencies help foster the development of products and services that can increase the company bottom line. Chief Diversity Officers of global organizations agree that a global mindset requires one to think about inclusion and diversity horizontally across various countries, borders, and cultures, and vertically by looking at intra- country cultural issues as well. One of the biggest mistakes American organizations have made in the past was to assume the "American way" would work with other cultures in countries around the world. Today, progressive global and multi-national organizations are building diversity and inclusion expectations based on the cultures within which they operate.

Technology has made the global workplace a reality, but our human behaviors are playing catch up to the capabilities of technology. I serve on the Global Speakers Federation Council. In this capacity, we conduct monthly leadership and committee meetings with the use of Skype. Something as simple as choosing the best time to meet is often quite a nightmare. If it is a good time for our North American members, it usually is not the best time for our Singapore and Australian members. Once on the call, we each must stay sensitive to the cultures represented so all points of view can be heard and considered.

My global clients share that global management of teams is one of the most rewarding responsibilities they have, and definitely one of the most challenging. To begin to develop your global diversity and inclusion skills, follow the same Four Cornerstones of Diversity Development discussed in chapter five: Knowledge, Understanding, Acceptance, and Behavior. Because there are so many books whose focus is totally on global diversity, I will not try to duplicate all the strategies and tactics here. Sometimes the best way to learn about others is to ask the right questions. Expand your development by answering to the following questions as you build your competencies:

How can I use technology to build my team and overcome the challenges of distance and time zones?
How can I learn the lessons of email, greetings, critical feedback and other nuances of working with people from many other countries?
What can I do to build individual relationships on a global platform?
How can I avoid appearing to be "the ugly American?"
What are the differences in interpretation of goals and deadlines across various cultures?
What are the differences in cultural expectations of men and women?
How are business decisions made cross culturally? (i.e. does "yes" really mean "yes.")
How much time must be committed to socializing and chit-chat

before I can get to the business?
Am I willing to flex my style?
Who do I know, or whom can I meet to help me navigate the
international mindset waters?

As you develop your skills with each individual consider where you
are and they are on the following socio-behavioral preferences scale.

Socio-Behavioral Preference

Socio-Behavioral Preferences

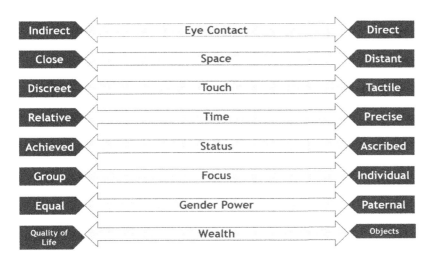

Bibliography and Reference List

Anderson, Redia and Lenora Billings-Harris. *Trailblazers: How Top Business Leaders are Accelerating Results through Inclusion and Diversity*. Hoboken, New Jersey: Wiley & Sons, 2010.

Barak, Michalle E. Mor. *Managing Diversity Toward a Globally Inclusive Workplace*. California: SAGE Publications, 2011.

Bucher, Richard D. and Patricia L. Bucher. *Diversity Consciousness: Opening our Minds to People, Cultures and Opportunities (3rd Edition)*. Prentice Hall, 2011.

Carr-Ruffino, Norma. *Managing Diversity: People Skills for a Multicultural Workplace*. New York: International Thomson, 1996.

Cox, Taylor, Jr. *Cultural Diversity in Organizations: Theory, Research and Practice*. San Francisco: Berrett-Koehler, 1993.

Cran, Cheryl. *101 Ways to Make Generations X, Y and Zoomers Happy At Work*. Synthesis at Work, 2010.

D'Amico, Carol, and Richard W. Judy. *Workforce 2020*. Hudson Institute, 1997.

Fernandez, John P. *Managing a Diverse Work Force: Regaining the Competitive Edge*. Lexington, Mass.: Lexington Books, 1991.

Gentile, Mary C. *Differences That Work: Organizational Excellence through Diversity*. Boston: Harvard Business School Press, 1994.

Hayles, Robert, and Armida Russell. *The Diversity Directive*. New York: McGraw Hill, 1997.

Hateley, Barbara, and Warren H. Schmidt. *A Peacock in the Land of Penguins: A Tale of Diversity and Discovery*. San Francisco: Berrett-Koehler, 1995.

Helminiak, Daniel A. *What the Bible Really Says About Homosexuality*. San Francisco: Alamo Square Press, 1995.

Johnston, William B., and Arnold H. Packer. *Workforce 2000*. New York: Hudson Institute, 1987.

Lee, Marlene and Mark Mather. *U.S. Labor Force Trends*. Population Bulletin, June, 2008.

Morrison, Terri and Wayne A. Conaway. *Kiss, Bow, or Shake Hands (The Bestselling Guide to Doing Business in More than 60 Countries)*. Adams Media, 2006. B000AR8BMW

Powers, Bob, and Alan Ellis. *A Manager's Guide to Sexual Orientation in the Workplace*. New York: Routledge, 1995.

Ross, Howard J. *Reinventing Diversity: Transforming Organizational Community to Strengthen People, Purpose, and Performance*. Rowman and Littlefield, 2011.

Sonnenschein, William. *Diversity Toolkit*. Illinois: NTC/Contemporary Publishing Group, Inc. 1999.

Swanton, Mary. *EEOC Wins Settlement in Two Age Discrimination Cases Involving Senior Citizens*. www.insidecounsel.com. <http:www.insidecounsel.com/2010/03/25/eeoc-wins-settlements-in-two-age-discrimination-cases-involving-senior-citizens>

Thiederman, Sondra, PhD. *Making Diversity Work*. New York: Kaplan Publishing, 2008.

Thomas, R. Roosevelt, Jr. *Beyond Race and Gender*. American Management Association, 1991.

Related Diversity
Word Definitions

Affirmative Action
Proactive actions taken to provide equal opportunity, as in admission of employment, development, and promotions, for under- represented groups such as people of color, women, and people with special needs.

Assimilation
When the dominant group becomes the standard of be- havior for all persons, and the majority expects members who are different to reject or repress their own culture and adopt the dominant culture in order to fit in. For example, in the past women were often expected to dress like men, so as not to distract men (the dominant group). Often rules are made simply for the comfort of the majority group rather than for clear business reasons.

Acculturation
A process used by organizations to help new members learn the values, customs, and norms of the organization. The goal is to focus the entire group on important organizational values without expecting those who are different to deny their own culture, while adapting to the organization's culture. For example, within many organizations men are allowed to have facial hair and wear an earring, and African American women can wear braids without feeling as though they are "bucking the system."

Ageism
Biases, opinions, and beliefs about individuals based solely on their age (young or old).

Ableism
Fear or discomfort regarding people with special needs. Inappropriate comments and gestures about people who are disabled.

Bias
An inclination or preference, especially one that interferes with impartial judgment.

Bigot
A person fanatically devoted to one's own group, religion, politics, or ethnic group and who is intolerant of those who differ.

Homophobia
The fear of homosexuals. Making anti-gay jokes and gestures. Believing it is acceptable to treat gays and lesbians and others who are not heterosexual as less than equal human beings, and to expect them to follow strict rules of conduct not expected of heterosexuals.

Inclusion
The process of including all types of people in the group or team, by recognizing that differences are an asset for achieving high productivity.

Multiculturalism
That which pertains to, or is designed for, several individual cultures or groups (i.e., the United States Constitution). For example, Disney and AT&T now recognize homosexual couples as equal to married couples for the purpose of employee benefits and health care, rather than denying them benefits just because they are different.

Prejudice
An adverse opinion or judgment formed beforehand or without full knowledge or complete examination of the facts. Irrational hatred or suspicion of a specific group or religion.

Pluralism
A condition of society in which numerous distinct ethnic, religious, cultural, or age groups coexist.

Sexism
Prejudice or discrimination based on gender, especially against women. Arbitrary stereotyping of social roles based on gender.

Stereotypes

A conventional, usually oversimplified opinion, perception, or belief about a person; lacking in individuality.

Racism

The notion that one's own ethnic stock is superior. Prejudice or discrimination based on ethnicity.

GIVE THE DIVERSITY ADVANTAGE THIRD EDITION
RESOURCES TO YOUR FRIENDS AND COLLEAGUES

About the Author

Lenora Billings-Harris

Diversity and Inclusion is a full-time focus, not just one topic among many for Lenora Billings-Harris. Whether through keynotes, virtual learning, or organizational consulting, Lenora partners with clients to help them build effective relationships that leverage diversity in order to increase inclusion, employee engagement, customer satisfaction and bottom-line results.

Billings-Harris is a recognized authority. She has been included as one of 100 Global Thought Leaders on Diversity and Inclusion by The Society of Human Resource Management (SHRM), and was named by Diversity Woman Magazine as one of the twenty top influential diversity leaders in the US. Her award winning diversity leadership research is recognized in academic journals internationally. Lenora is called upon by leaders in large and small organizations across the globe, including South Africa and Israel to share best practices within business, government, education and NGO communities.

Billings-Harris is often an expert guest on TV and radio around the globe. She serves on the adjunct faculty of the business schools of Averett University and the University of North Carolina-Greensboro.

Lenora is an active leader within her profession. She earned the highest speaking designation, the Certified Speaking Professional (CSP) in 1997, and was president of the National Speakers Association for 2006-2007 . She is the 2014-2015 president of the Global Speakers Federation, and was inducted as one of the Legends of the Speaking Profession in 2014. Before launching her business in 1986, she held management positions at two Fortune 100 companies, and managed executive development seminars for the Graduate School of Business, University of Michigan.

For more information, event bookings and interviews Contact:

Ubuntu Global
PO Box 1628
Greensboro NC 27402
USA

Reach or Follow Lenora

Website: www.UbuntuGlobal.com

Blog: www.GlobalDiversityTalk.com

Webinars: www.BeyondthePlatform.com

Email: Info@UbuntuGlobal.com

Skype: DiversityLBH

Twitter: @LBHdiversity

YouTube: www.youtube.com/user/lenorabillingsharris

Take the Ubuntu Pledge http://goo.gl/c3k4EV

Video: http://vimeo.com/74461209

The Diversity Advantage ebook version: http://goo.gl/9q6f5d

Trailblazers hardcover
　　　　http://lenorabillingsharris.com/abouttrailblazers

The Diversity Advantage

This easy to read book is filled with reality-based applications that will help you lead and work with today's diverse teams, clients and customers."

— Harvey Mackay, author of the New York Times #1 bestseller
Swim With the Sharks Without Being Eaten Alive

Lenora's STOP technique (detailed in this book) is a fast and simple way to give diversity-related feedback at home or in the workplace. A great resource for workshops, and supervisory training.

— Craig E. Philip, CEO Ingram Barge Company

Billings-Harris has drawn from her vast experience to provide us with a valuable collection of perceptions and strategies that will enhance any diversity effort. Keep this book at your fingertips for the unlimited insights it provides!

— Howard Ross, Cook Ross, Inc.
Author, *ReInventing Diversity: Transforming Organizational Community to Strengthen People, Purpose, and Performance*

Lenora Billings-Harris transforms a complex topic into easy to follow, solutions. The Diversity Advantage is informative, comprehensive, and concise. With scenarios, examples, and definitions, this book provides clarity to diversity in our times.

—Amy Kahn, PhD, Director of Diversity,
University of the Rockies

Ms. Billings-Harris helps leaders go beyond diversity awareness. The Diversity Advantage illustrates how to develop the skills needed to be an engaged leader of all types of diverse teams here and abroad. This is a must have resource for executives, HR professionals and learning professionals.

— Sheila Robinson, Publisher, Diversity Woman Magazine

There is no greater time to appreciate the lessons of the Diversity Advantage. In this third edition, Lenora continues to capture the essence of the challenges we all face in better understanding each other in order to be more effective leaders, team members, teachers, and students. Diversity can be an advantage or our undoing, the choice is ours.

— Lee Finkel, Vice President of Academic Administration,
University of Phoenix